Street by Street

YORK
TADCASTER
Bishopthorpe, Copmanthorpe, Dunnington, Haxby, Heslington, Nether Poppleton, Skelton, Stamford Bridge, Strensall

GAZETTEER SYMBOL KEY

- ☎ - telephone number
- ✆ - telephone booking service
- @ - email address
- 🖱 - web address
- 📠 - fax number
-  - map page number and grid reference

1st edition published July 2008
© Automobile Association Developments Limited 2008

This product includes map data licensed from Ordnance Survey® with the permission of the Controller of Her Majesty's Stationery Office.
© Crown copyright 2008.
All rights reserved. Licence number 100021153.

The copyright in all PAF is owned by Royal Mail Group plc.

All rights reserved. No part of this publication may be reproduced, stored in a retrieval system, or transmitted in any form or by any means – electronic, mechanical, photocopying, recording or otherwise – unless the permission of the publisher has been given beforehand.

Published by AA Publishing (a trading name of Automobile Association Developments Limited, whose registered office is Fanum House, Basing View, Basingstoke, Hampshire RG21 4EA. Registered number 1878835).

Cartography produced by the Mapping Services Department of The Automobile Association. (A03534)

A CIP Catalogue record for this book is available from the British Library.

Design and management for listings section by ey communications Ltd. (www.eysite.com). Editorial services by Pam Stagg

Listings data provided by Global DataPoint Limited, London

Printed by Oriental Press in Dubai

The Automobile Association would like to thank the following photographers, companies and picture libraries for their assistance in the preparation of this book.

Abbreviations for the picture credits are as follows: (t) top; (b) bottom; (l) left; (r) right; (AA) AA World Travel Library.
Front Cover AA/P Bennett;
3 (t) AA/R Newton; 3 (ct) AA; 3 (cb) AA/P Bennett; 3 (b) AA/R Newton

Every effort has been made to trace the copyright holders and we apologise in advance for any accidental errors. We would be happy to apply the corrections in the following edition of this publication.

The contents of this atlas are believed to be correct at the time of the latest revision. However, the publishers cannot be held responsible or liable for any loss or damage occasioned to any person acting or refraining from action as a result of any use or reliance on any material in this atlas, nor for any errors, omissions or changes in such material. This does not affect your statutory rights. The publishers would welcome information to correct any errors or omissions and to keep this atlas up to date. Please write to Publishing, The Automobile Association, Fanum House (FH12), Basing View, Basingstoke, Hampshire RG21 4EA.
Email: *streetbystreet@theaa.com*

Ref: ML154z

Opposite page
Top: York Guildhall on the banks of the River Ouse
Centre top: Street entertainers in The Shambles
Centre bottom: York Minster, the city's crowning glory
Bottom: The White Rose of York is the city's emblem

York...

The historic city of York, on the banks of the River Ouse, has countless visitor attractions and hosts an exciting and diverse year-round programme of festivals. As much of the city's compact heart is pedestrianised, it's a great place to explore on foot – a circuit of the medieval walls is an excellent way to get your bearings. River cruises, open-top bus tours and guided evening ghost walks offer an alternative perspective of the city.

Two of the most popular shopping streets are The Shambles, a short, narrow street of timber-framed medieval buildings, and Stonegate, which is filled with street entertainers. This is where you'll find Ye Old Starre Inne, one of the historic pubs tucked away in the city's ancient snickelways.

To help you make the most of your leisure time in York we have provided a useful gazetteer covering a range of attractions from outstanding museums and art galleries, to cinemas and grand theatres featuring everything from opera to live music and classical ballet. There are historic pubs hidden away in the city's snickelways and trendy bars featuring live music at weekends along with the cocktails.

Entries are listed alphabetically (ignoring The) under each category heading. The map reference at the end of each entry denotes the map page number in the mapping section and the grid square in which the street/road is to be found, not the individual establishments. We have given the street name, town/city name, post code, telephone and fax numbers and, where possible, email and website details.

Please note: the entries listed in this gazetteer section were provided by a third party and are not in any way recommended or endorsed by the AA.

TOURIST ATTRACTIONS

Barley Hall

Barley Hall is a medieval building in the centre of the city which was revealed during excavations in 1980s. The Hall was home to Alderman William Snawsell, goldsmith and Mayor of York. The restored building's roof is covered with replica medieval tiles made by the potter John Hudson, and the floor depicts the original layings and pattern with contemporary illustrations.

2 Coffee Yard, Stonegate, York, North Yorkshire YO1 8AR
- ☎ 01904 610275
- @ barley.hall@btconnect.com
- www.barleyhall.org.uk
- Page 3-F3

Derwent Valley Light Railway

The Derwent Valley Light Railway began in its current form in 1989 and operates train services on the remaining section of the original Derwent Valley Railway. Services run throughout the summer, from Easter until September on Sundays and Bank Holidays, in addition to Santa Special trains in December.

Murton Park, Murton Lane, York, North Yorkshire YO19 5UF
- ☎ 01904 489966
- @ dvlr@hotmail.co.uk
- www.dvlr.org.uk
- Page 20-C4

English Heritage: The Archaeological Resource Centre

The Archaeological Resource Centre allows visitors to become an archaeologist and handle real ancient artefacts, piecing together the past and finding out what life was like centuries ago.

St Saviour's Church, St Saviourgate, York, North Yorkshire YO1 8NN
- ☎ 01904 643211, 01904 654324
- @ jorvik@yorkarchaeology.co.uk
- www.english-heritage.org.uk/server/show/ConProperty.398
- Page 3-G4

English Heritage: Clifford's Tower

Clifford's Tower, a proud symbol of the might of England's medieval kings, enjoys sweeping views of the city. The original wooden tower was built to help William the Conqueror subdue the North. It was burned down during the persecution of the Jewish community in 1190 and rebuilt in a rare design of interlocking circles by Henry III in the 13th century.

Clifford's Tower, York, North Yorkshire YO1 9SA
- ☎ 01904 646940
- www.english-heritage.org.uk
- Page 3-F6

English Heritage: Merchant Adventurers Hall

The Merchant Adventurer's Hall was built between 1357 and 1361 and features collections of paintings, furniture and silver from the bygone periods.

Fossgate, York, North Yorkshire YO1 9XD
- ☎ 01904 654818
- @ enquiries@theyorkcompany.co.uk
- www.theyorkcompany.co.uk
- 01904 616150
- Page 3-G4

Fairfax House

Fairfax House is an 18th-century house in the North of England and features a kitchen, saloon, bedroom and drawing room besides housing the late Noel Terry's collection of Georgian furniture.

Castlegate, York, North Yorkshire YO1 9RN
- ☎ 01904 655543
- @ info@fairfaxhouse.co.uk
- www.fairfaxhouse.co.uk
- 01904 652262
- Page 3-F5

Jorvik Viking Centre

Jorvik brings alive a shadowy era in the history of York and the nation. It was created by York Archaeological Trust on the site of the Viking dig that it carried out here in Coppergate between 1976 and 1981. Jorvik shows how much archaeology contributes to the discovery and understanding of the past. Here you can encounter Viking residents, learn what life was like here 1,000 years ago and journey through a reconstruction of actual Viking streets.

15–17 Coppergate, York, North Yorkshire YO1 9WT
- ☎ 01904 543403, 01904 543400
- @ jorvik@yorkarchaeology.co.uk
- www.jorvik-viking-centre.co.uk/index2.htm
- 01904 627097
- Page 3-F5

National Trust: Goddards Garden

The former home of Noel Goddard Terry of the York chocolate making firm, the house was designed in 1927 by Walter Brierley. The garden, designed by George Dillistone, features terraces, a rockery, ponds, borders and a collection of shrubs.

27 Tadcaster Road, York, North Yorkshire YO24 1GG
- ☎ 01904 702021
- @ goddardsgarden@nationaltrust.org.uk
- www.nationaltrust.org.uk
- Page 23-G3

National Trust: Treasurer's House

Treasurer's House was originally home to the treasurers of York Minster. The House, built over a Roman road, was restored between 1897 and 1930 by a local industrialist Frank Green, with rooms presented in a variety of historic styles. The ghosts of a Roman legion reputedly march through the cellars and displays include a ship made out of bones.

Minster Yard, York, North Yorkshire YO1 7JL
- ☎ 01904 624247
- @ treasurershouse@nationaltrust.org.uk
- www.nationaltrust.org.uk

Tourist Attractions - Museums

☎ 01904 647372
 Page 3-F2

The York Dungeon
The dungeon lies deep in the heart of historic York, buried beneath its very paving stones. It brings alive about 2,000 years of history and death.

12 Clifford Street, York, North Yorkshire YO1 9RD
☎ 01904 632599
@ york.dungeons@merlin entertainments.biz
 www.thedungeons.com
 01904 612602
 Page 3-F5

York Minster
York Minster stands at the very centre of England's religious and political life. A tour of the minster features the Undercroft, Treasury and Crypt as well as the Central Tower.

St Williams College, 4–5 College Street, York, North Yorkshire YO1 7JF
☎ 01904 557216
@ info@yorkminster.org
 www.yorkminster.org
 01904 557201
 Page 3-F3

MUSEUMS

The Bar Convent Museum
The Bar Convent is steeped in history and is the oldest living Catholic convent in England. In 1686 Frances Bedingfield, a member of Mary Ward's Institute (founded in 1609) came with a small group of nuns to purchase a modest 17th-century house standing outside Micklegate Bar and the city walls. A fascinating museum brings to life the history of the Bar Convent and religion in the North of England.

17 Blossom Street, York, North Yorkshire YO24 1AQ
☎ 01904 643238
@ info@bar-convent.org.uk
 www.bar-convent.org.uk
 01904 631792
 Page 2-D6

English Heritage: Merchant Adventurers Hall
The Merchant Adventurer's Hall was built between 1357 and 1361 and features collections of paintings, furniture and silver from the bygone periods.

Fossgate, York, North Yorkshire YO1 9XD
☎ 01904 654818
@ enquiries@theyorkcompany.co.uk
 www.theyorkcompany.co.uk
 01904 616150
 Page 3-G4

Kohima Museum
The collection commemorates the Battle of Kohima in north east India and follows the fortunes of the 2nd Division up to and including its role in crossing the Irrawady.

Imphal Barracks, Fulford Road, York, North Yorkshire YO1 4AU
☎ 01904 665806, 01904 635212
@ thekohimamuseum@hotmail.com
 www.armymuseums.org.uk/index.htm
 01904 662655
 Page 24-C3

Micklegate Bar Museum
Micklegate Bar has a range of exhibits covering over 800 years using models, skulls, and displays as realistic looking and as accurate as possible. The Museum portrays the history of York and looks at families who once lived here. You can see just how heavy real chain mail armour is, try on soldiers' helmets, meet the Royalist defender, examine the old prisoner cell, and much more.

Micklegate, York, North Yorkshire YO1 6JX
☎ 01904 634436, 01904 792445
@ micklegate.bar@clara.net
 www.micklegatebar.co.uk
 Page 2-C6

National Railway Museum
The National Railway Museum in York, England, is the largest railway museum in the world, responsible for the conservation and interpretation of the British national collection of historically significant railway vehicles and other artefacts. The Museum contains an unrivalled collection of locomotives, rolling stock, railway equipment, documents and records.

Leeman Road, York, North Yorkshire YO26 4XJ
☎ 0870 421 4001
@ nrm@nrm.org.uk
 www.nrm.org.uk
 01904 611112
 Page 2-B4

Prince of Wales's Own Regiment of Yorkshire
3 Tower Street, York, North Yorkshire YO1 9SB
☎ 01904 662790
@ yorksregtaffairs@btconnect.com
 www.yorkshireregiment.mod.uk
 Page 3-F5

The Regimental Museum of the Royal Dragoon Guards
The Museum is set in spacious surroundings and tells the story of the present day and former regiments from the late 17th century. Displays include uniforms, prints, paintings, weapons and Standards, all housed in well-lit, clearly labelled show cases.

3a Tower Street, York, North Yorkshire YO1 9SB
☎ 01904 642036
@ hhq@rdgmuseum.org.uk
 www.rdgmuseum.org.uk
 Page 3-F5

Richard III Museum
Possibly one of York's best kept secrets, this fascinating museum is situated in York's tallest and most impressive medieval gatehouse – Monk Bar. Built in the 14th century as part of York's famous city walls, it was originally a guardhouse and has been both a prison and a police house, and was lived in until 1914.

Monk Bar, York, North Yorkshire YO1 7LQ

Museums – Dance and Performing Arts

☎ 01904 634191
@ info@richardiiimuseum.co.uk
⌂ www.richard3museum.co.uk
▸ Page 3-G3

York Castle Museum
York Castle Museum is one of Britain's leading museums of everyday life. It shows how people used to live by displaying thousands of household objects and by recreating rooms, shops, streets and even prison cells.

Eye of York, York, North Yorkshire YO1 9RY
☎ 01904 687687
⌂ www.yorkcastlemuseum.org.uk/Page/YorkCastleMuseum.aspx
▸ Page 3-G6

Yorkshire Museum and Gardens
Yorkshire Museum and Gardens houses Roman and Viking finds, as well as internationally renowned collections of pottery and fossils.

Yorkshire Museum, Museum Gardens, York, North Yorkshire YO1 7FR
☎ 01904 687687
@ yorkshire.museum@ymt.org.uk
⌂ www.yorkshiremuseum.org.uk
▸ Page 2-D3

Yorkshire Museum of Farming
The Yorkshire Museum of Farming holds a fantastic regional agricultural collection. Displays give a detailed look at how agriculture has shaped and influenced both society and the landscape. The collection includes many thousands of objects, photographs and archival material dedicated to the tools and techniques that have produced our daily bread for over 250 years.

Murton Park, Murton Lane, York, North Yorkshire YO19 5UF
☎ 01904 489966
⌂ www.murtonpark.co.uk/html/farming_museum.html
▸ Page 20-C4

ART GALLERIES AND VISUAL ARTS

Kentmere House Gallery
Kentmere House Gallery displays paintings and original prints by Britain's living artists. The gallery specialises in promoting the work of talented and promising newcomers alongside that of established artists.

53 Scarcroft Hill, York, North Yorkshire YO24 1DF
☎ 01904 656507
@ ann@kentmerehouse.co.uk
⌂ www.kentmerehouse.co.uk
▸ Page 23-H2

Minster Fine Art Gallery
The exhibition space showcases original collectable works by established artists. Paintings, monoprints, sculpture and studio ceramics are represented in a programme of changing exhibitions that complement works by the gallery's permanent artists.

The Old Convent, The Queen's Path, 7 Minster Yard, York, North Yorkshire YO1 7JD
☎ 01904 658721
@ info@minsterfineart.co.uk
⌂ www.minsterfineart.co.uk
▸ Page 3-F3

Pyramid Gallery
Pyramid Gallery offers British made contemporary crafts, jewellery and original prints. Selected for quality by the Crafts Council, the gallery displays work by many leading designers and makers who work in glass, ceramics, wood and metal.

43 Stonegate, York, North Yorkshire YO1 8AW
☎ 01904 641187
@ pyramidgallery7@yahoo.co.uk
⌂ www.pyramidgallery.com
▸ Page 2-E4

York Art Gallery
The gallery hosts a collection of British and European art spanning the last 600 years, which is displayed in themed areas under the headings of people, places, stories, devotion and morality. Changing displays from these collections are complemented by a programme of temporary exhibitions and events.

Exhibition Square, York, North Yorkshire YO1 7EW
☎ 01904 687687
@ art.gallery@ymt.org.uk
⌂ www.yorkartgallery.org.uk
▸ Page 2-D2

York College
Art & Design Foyer, York, North Yorkshire YO1 7EW
☎ 01904 770277/658721
⌂ www.yorkcollege.ac.uk/news/exhibitions.htm
▸ Page 27-G2

York St Marys
York St Mary's is a former church which is now a contemporary art venue run by York Museums Trust. Each year the trust commissions an artist to create a piece of art within this unique space. This fine medieval church has the tallest spire in York at 47 metres high. An inscription within the church suggests it could have been consecrated as early as 1020, but very little of the original Saxon church remains. The bulk of the building dates to the early 13th century, with 14th- and 15th-century additions including the octagonal tower and spire.

Castlegate, York, North Yorkshire YO1 9RN
☎ 01904 650333, 01904 687687
⌂ www.yorkstmarys.org.uk
▸ Page 3-F5

DANCE AND PERFORMING ARTS

York Theatre Royal
The theatre hosts a wide range of events such as drama, comedy, dance, pantomime and youth theatre.

St Leonard's Place, York, North Yorkshire YO1 7HD
☎ 01904 658162
✆ 01904 623568
@ marketing@yorktheatreroyal.co.uk
⌂ www.yorktheatreroyal.co.uk
📄 01904 550164
▸ Page 2-E3

Live Music Venues - Cinemas

LIVE MUSIC VENUES

The Black Swan Inn
Peasholme Green, York, North Yorkshire YO1 7PR
☎ 01904 686911
@ mike@yorkblackswan.fsnet.co.uk
🔗 www.blackswanyork.co.uk
📄 Page 3-H4

Fibbers
Fibbers offers live music of every type, every night of the week from local to national circuit acts.

Stonebow House, The Stonebow, York, North Yorkshire YO1 7NP
☎ 01904 651250
@ fibbers@fibbers.co.uk
🔗 www.fibbers.co.uk
📄 01904 651250
📄 Page 3-G4

COMEDY CLUBS AND VENUES

York Theatre Royal
The theatre hosts a wide range of events such as drama, comedy, dance, pantomime and youth theatre.

St Leonard's Place, York, North Yorkshire YO1 7HD
☎ 01904 658162
☎ 01904 623568
@ marketing@yorktheatreroyal.co.uk
🔗 www.yorktheatreroyal.co.uk
📄 01904 550164
📄 Page 2-E3

CLASSICAL MUSIC VENUES

Bedern Hall
Bartle Garth, St Andrewgate, York, North Yorkshire YO1 7AL
☎ 01904 653698
@ info@bedernhall.co.uk
🔗 www.bedernhall.co.uk/
📄 Page 3-G3

Chapter House
Minster Yard, York, North Yorkshire YO1 7HH
☎ 01423 521316
@ enquiries@chapterhousechoir.org
🔗 www.chapterhousechoir.org
📄 Page 3-F3

National Centre For Early Music
The events programme includes early music, jazz, folk, world, contemporary and classical music.

St Margarets Churh, Walmgate, York, North Yorkshire YO1 9TL
☎ 01904 632220
📞 01904 658338
@ info@ncem.co.uk
🔗 www.ncem.co.uk
📄 01904 612631
📄 Page 3-H5

Sir Jack Lyons Concert Hall
Most of the university's concerts are held in Sir Jack Lyons Concert Hall in the Department of Music but major choral and orchestral concerts take place in the Central Hall of the University or in York Minster. Concerts take place on Wednesday evenings, and on some Friday and Saturday evenings, during term time.

All concerts are open to members of the public. All venues have access and facilities for people with disabilities.

Department of Music, University of York, Heslington, York, North Yorkshire YO10 5DD
☎ 01904 432439
@ boxoffice@york.ac.uk
🔗 www.yorkconcerts.co.uk
📄 Page 25-E2

St Mary's, Haxby
St Mary's is an Anglican Christian church within the Church of England Deanery of York which is part of the Diocese of York. Hosts various music events.

The Village, Haxby, York, North Yorkshire YO32 2JG
☎ 01904 760455
@ editor@haxbystmarys.org
🔗 www.haxbystmarys.org
📄 Page 6-C2

St Olave's Church
The Parish Church of St Olave's in the ancient city of York has the distinction of being the most ancient foundation in the British Isles dedicated in honour of Olaf King of Norway. There was a church on this site within three decades of his death at the battle of Stiklestad in the 11th century. From that church grew the Benedictine Community who built and occupied St Mary's Abbey until the dissolution of the monasteries. Hosts music events.

30 Marygate, York, North Yorkshire YO30 7BH
☎ 01904 627401
@ sharon.whittington@stolave.org.uk
🔗 www.stolave.org.uk
📄 Page 2-D3

Unitarian Chapel
St Saviourgate Chapel, York, Nrth Yorkshire YO1 8NQ
☎ 07946 487321
@ yorkunitarians@hotmail.co.uk
🔗 www.yorkunitarians.org.uk/
📄 Page 3-F4

CINEMAS

City Screen Picturehouse
The cinema has three auditoria, the largest is equipped to the prestigious THX standard. All screens have modern and very comfortable seating.

13–17 Coney Street, York, North Yorkshire YO1 9QL
☎ 0870 758 3219
@ cityscreenyork@picturehouses.co.uk
🔗 www.picturehouses.co.uk
📄 01904 541166
📄 Page 2-E4

Vue York
Clifton Moor Centre, Stirling Road, York, North Yorkshire YO30 4XY
☎ 08712 240240
@ customerservices@vuemail.com
🔗 www.myvue.com
📄 Page 9-G3

Theatres – Special Events' Venues

THEATRES

Chapel Theatre
St Johns College, Lord Mayors Walk, York, North Yorkshire YO31 7EX
☎ 01904 624624
🖰 www2.yorksj.ac.uk/
➤ Page 3-F1

Friargate Theatre
Friargate Theatre became the Riding Lights Theatre Company's first permanent home in 1999. The Company presents its latest productions regularly to the local community of York, and its many visitors.
Lower Friargate, York, North Yorkshire YO1 9SL
☎ 01904 655317
@ info@rltc.org
🖰 www.ridinglights.org
▤ 01904 651532
➤ Page 3-F5

Grand Opera House
This is Yorkshire's biggest theatre and the home of live entertainment in the region. Grand Opera House plays host to some of the biggest names from the entertainment world and rock and pop.
Cumberland Street, York, North Yorkshire YO1 9SW
☎ 0870 606 3595
🖰 www.grandoperahouseyork.org.uk
➤ Page 3-F5

Joseph Rowntree Theatre
The Joseph Rowntree Theatre is a volunteer-run theatre near the centre of York, which provides a venue for amateur and professional theatre, dance, music and other stage based events. A wide and varied range of shows are put on in the theatre, mainly by local amateur organisations with a few visiting professional events.
Haxby Road, York, North Yorkshire YO91 1RT
☎ 01904 658197
@ publicity@jrtheatre.co.uk
🖰 www.jrtheatre.co.uk
➤ Page 18-C1

York Theatre Royal
The theatre hosts a wide range of events such as drama, comedy, dance, pantomime and youth theatre.
St Leonard's Place, York, North Yorkshire YO1 7HD
☎ 01904 658162
📞 01904 623568
@ marketing@yorktheatreroyal.co.uk
🖰 www.yorktheatreroyal.co.uk
▤ 01904 550164
➤ Page 2-E3

BARS AND PUBS

Dusk
An independent and trendy bar with a large second floor for live music and DJs.
8 New Street, York, North Yorkshire YO1 8RA
☎ 01904 634851
➤ Page 2-E4

The Living Room, York
The Living Room in York boasts fabulous views across the River Ouse and has become a favourite neighbourhood hangout in the city centre.
Merchant Exchange, 1 Bridge Street, York, North Yorkshire YO1 6DD
☎ 01904 461000
@ york@thelivingroom.co.uk
🖰 www.thelivingroom.co.uk
▤ 01904 628967
➤ Page 2-E5

Old White Swan
80 Goodramgate, York, North Yorkshire YO1 7LF
☎ 01904 540911
➤ Page 3-F4

The Punch Bowl
7 Stonegate, York, North Yorkshire YO1 8AN
☎ 01904 615491
➤ Page 2-E4

Stone Roses Bar
4 King Street, York, North Yorkshire YO1 9SP
☎ 01904 670696
🖰 www.stonerosesbar.com
➤ Page 3-F5

NIGHTCLUBS

The Gallery Nightclub
12 Clifford Street, York, North Yorkshire YO1 1RD
☎ 01904 647947
@ www.galleryclub.co.uk
▤ 01904 671113
➤ Page 3-F5

The Junction York
Leeman Road, York, North Yorkshire YO26 4XH
☎ 01904 639979
@ thejunction.york@gmail.com
➤ Page 2-C4

Toffs
Toffs nightclub offers live bands and DJs across a wide genre of music including hip hop, rock, indie, R'n'B and other club classics.
3–5 Toft Green, York, North Yorkshire YO1 6JT
☎ 01904 620203
@ toffs-york@luminar.co.uk
🖰 www.toffsnightclub.co.uk
▤ 01904 613592
➤ Page 2-D5

Ziggys
53–55 Micklegate, York, North Yorkshire YO1 6LJ
☎ 01904 620602
@ contact@ziggysnightclub.com
🖰 www.ziggysnightclub.com/
➤ Page 2-E5

SPECIAL EVENTS' VENUES

The Ice Factor: York's Christmas Ice Rink
Set against the backdrop of Clifford's Tower in the centre of York, the 600-square metre rink of ice enjoys one of the most picturesque settings in the country for outdoor skating. The ice-skating area also includes York's biggest Christmas tree, log cabins, theatrical lighting and the oak tree in the centre of the rink sparkling with fairy lights.
York City Centre, York, North Yorkshire YO1 9RY
☎ 01653 619169
@ admin@theicefactor.co.uk
🖰 www.theicefactor.co.uk
➤ Page 3-F6

Street by Street

YORK
TADCASTER
Bishopthorpe, Copmanthorpe, Dunnington, Haxby, Heslington, Nether Poppleton, Skelton, Stamford Bridge, Strensall

Key to map pages	ii-iii
Key to map symbols	iv-1
Enlarged map pages	2-3
Main map pages	4-31
Index – towns & villages	32
Index – streets	33-40
Index – featured places	40-41
Acknowledgements	41

Enlarged scale pages **1:10,000** **6.3 inches to 1 mile**

0 1/4 miles 1/2

0 1/4 1/2 kilometres 3/4 1

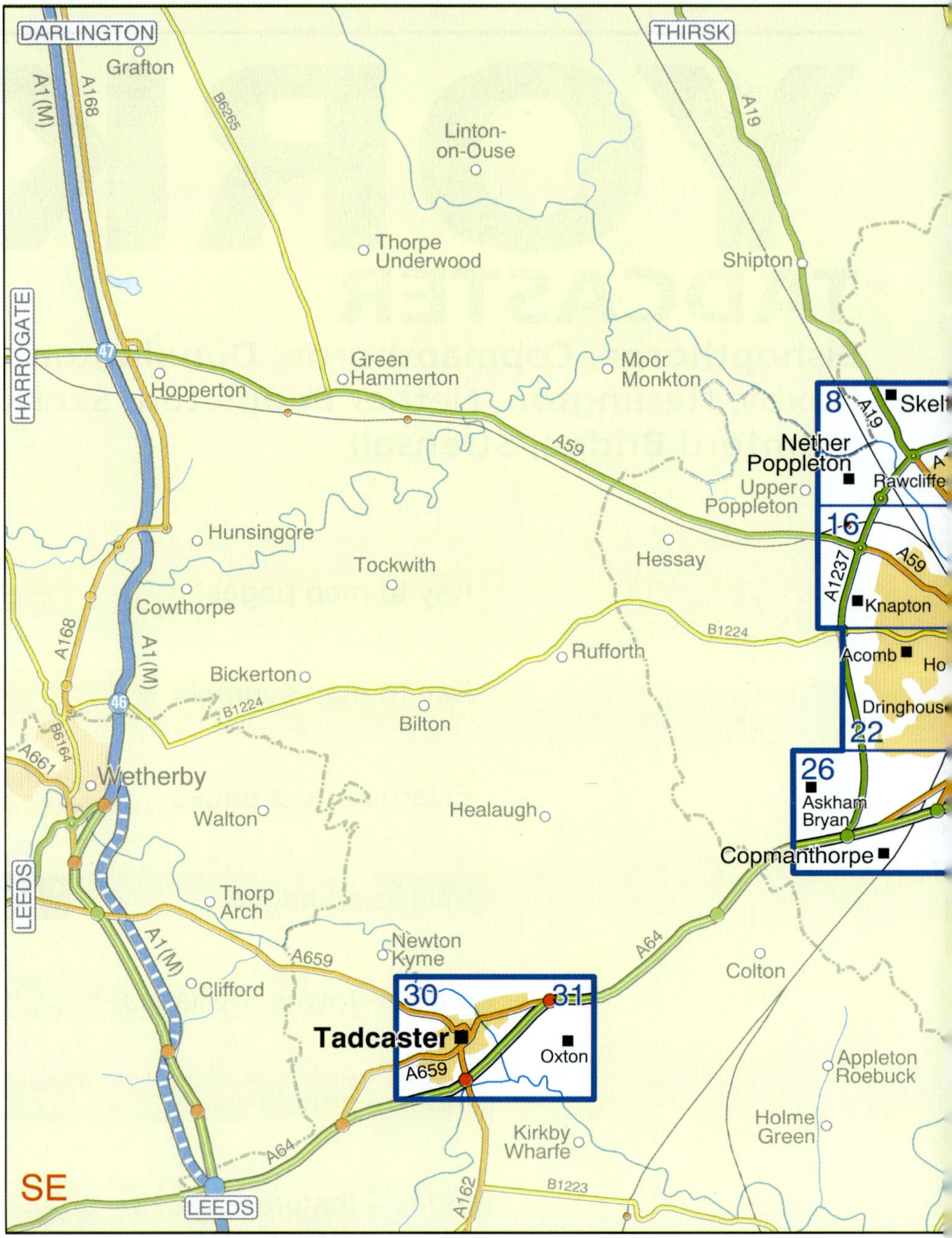

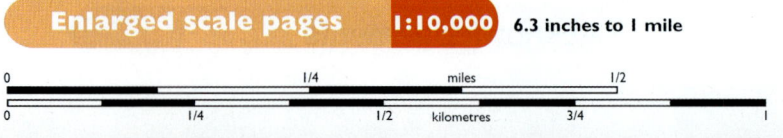

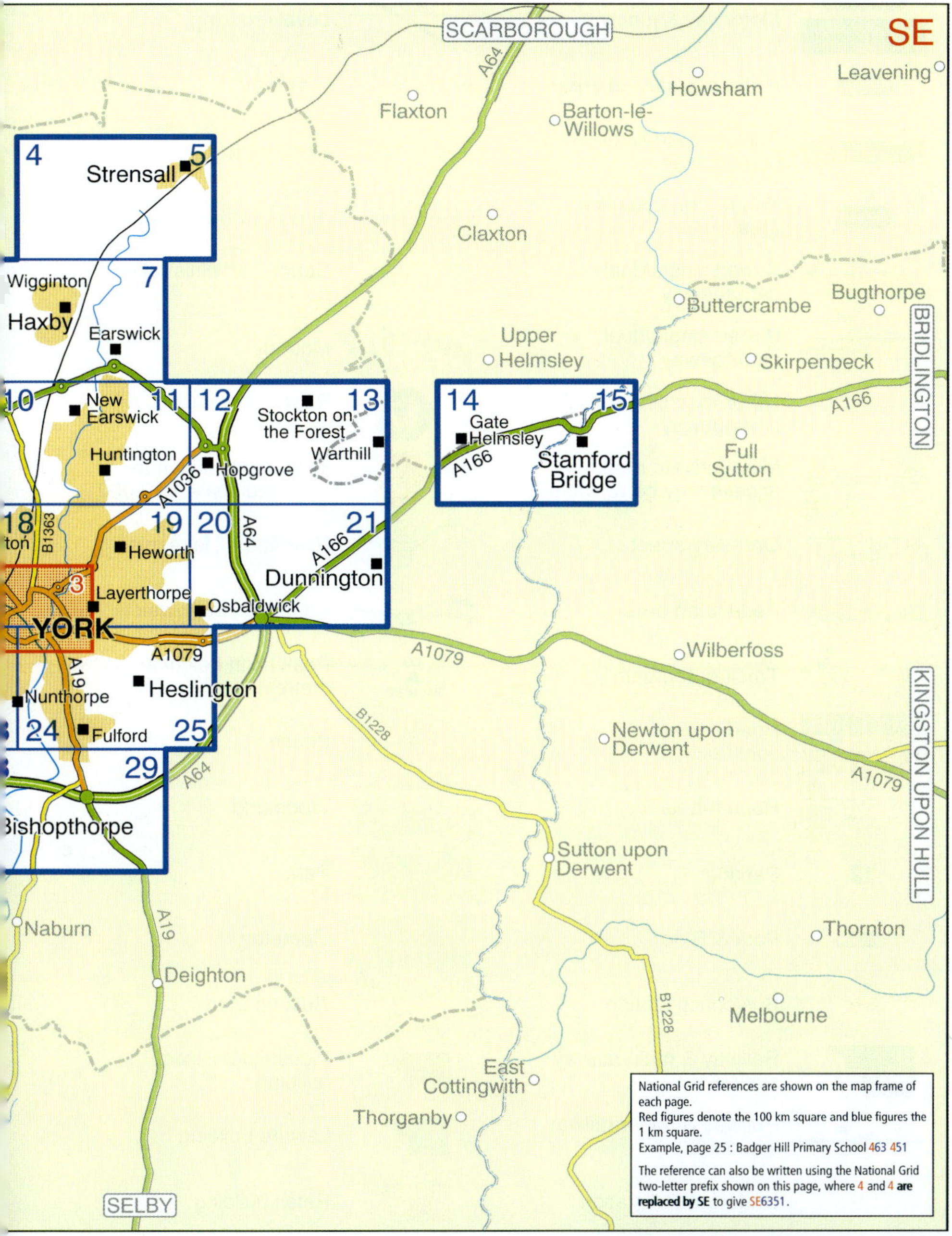

Key to Map Pages & Routeplanner iii

SE

National Grid references are shown on the map frame of each page.
Red figures denote the 100 km square and blue figures the 1 km square.
Example, page 25 : Badger Hill Primary School **463** 451
The reference can also be written using the National Grid two-letter prefix shown on this page, where **4** and **4** are replaced by **SE** to give SE6351.

4.2 inches to 1 mile   **Scale of main map pages 1:15,000**

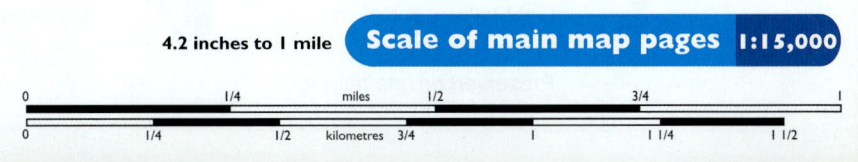

Symbol	Description	Symbol	Description
Junction 9	Motorway & junction	LC	Level crossing
Services	Motorway service area		Tramway
	Primary road single/dual carriageway		Ferry route
Services	Primary road service area		Airport runway
	A road single/dual carriageway		County, administrative boundary
	B road single/dual carriageway		Mounds
	Other road single/dual carriageway	17	Page continuation 1:15,000
	Minor/private road, access may be restricted	3	Page continuation to enlarged scale 1:10,000
	One-way street		River/canal, lake, pier
	Pedestrian area		Aqueduct, lock, weir
	Track or footpath	465 ▲ Winter Hill	Peak (with height in metres)
	Road under construction		Beach
	Road tunnel		Woodland
P	Parking		Park
P+	Park & Ride		Cemetery
	Bus/coach station		Built-up area
	Railway & main railway station		Industrial/business building
	Railway & minor railway station		Leisure building
	Underground station		Retail building
	Light railway & station		Other building
	Preserved private railway		

Map Symbols

Symbol	Description	Symbol	Description
ᴨᴨᴨᴨᴨ	City wall		Castle
A&E	Hospital with 24-hour A&E department		Historic house or building
PO	Post Office	Wakehurst Place NT	National Trust property
	Public library	M	Museum or art gallery
i	Tourist Information Centre		Roman antiquity
i	Seasonal Tourist Information Centre		Ancient site, battlefield or monument
	Petrol station, 24 hour Major suppliers only		Industrial interest
†	Church/chapel		Garden
	Public toilets		Garden Centre Garden Centre Association Member
	Toilet with disabled facilities		Garden Centre Wyevale Garden Centre
PH	Public house AA recommended		Arboretum
	Restaurant AA inspected		Farm or animal centre
Madeira Hotel	Hotel AA inspected		Zoological or wildlife collection
	Theatre or performing arts centre		Bird collection
	Cinema		Nature reserve
	Golf course		Aquarium
▲	Camping AA inspected	V	Visitor or heritage centre
	Caravan site AA inspected		Country park
▲	Camping & caravan site AA inspected		Cave
	Theme park		Windmill
	Abbey, cathedral or priory		Distillery, brewery or vineyard

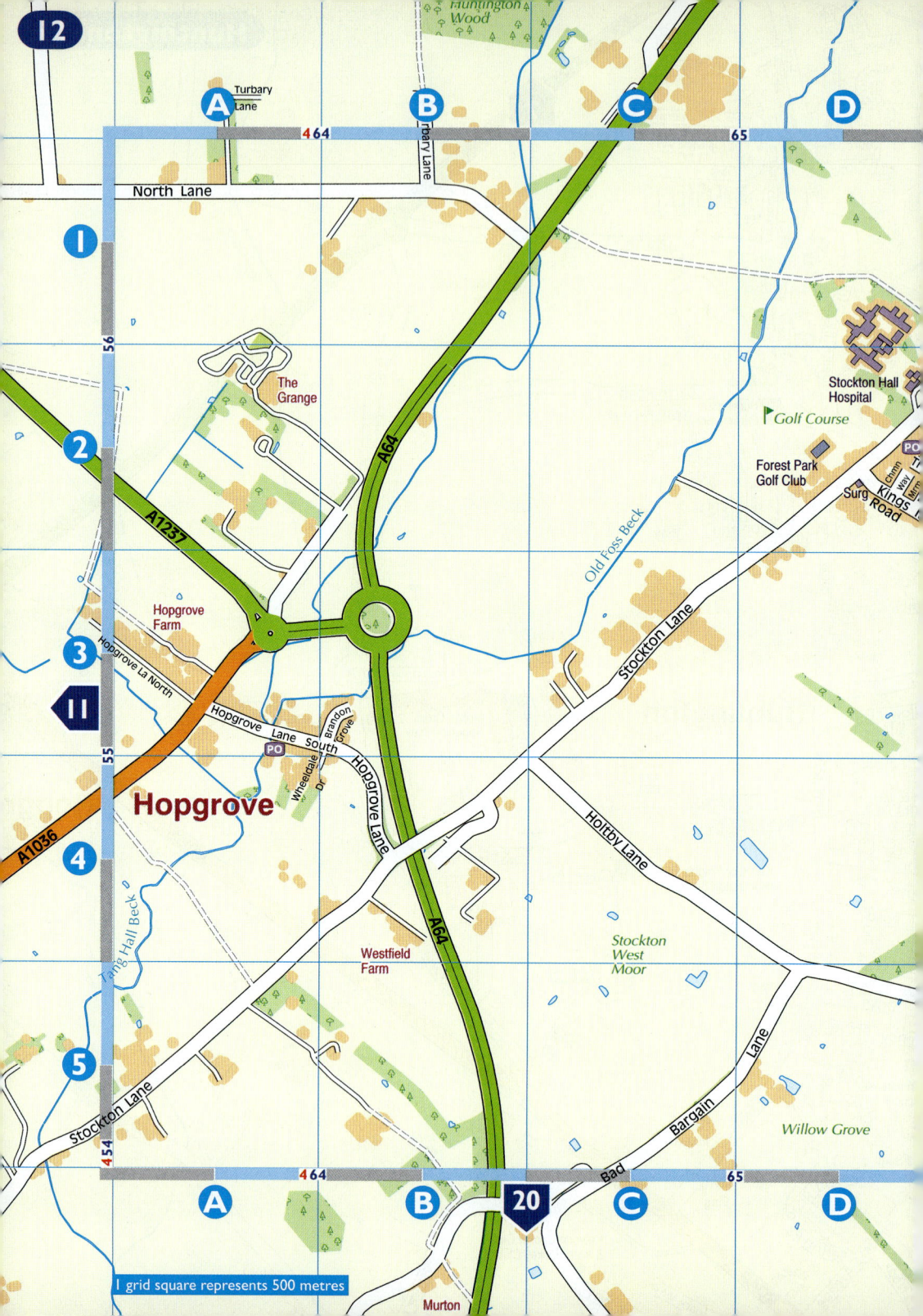

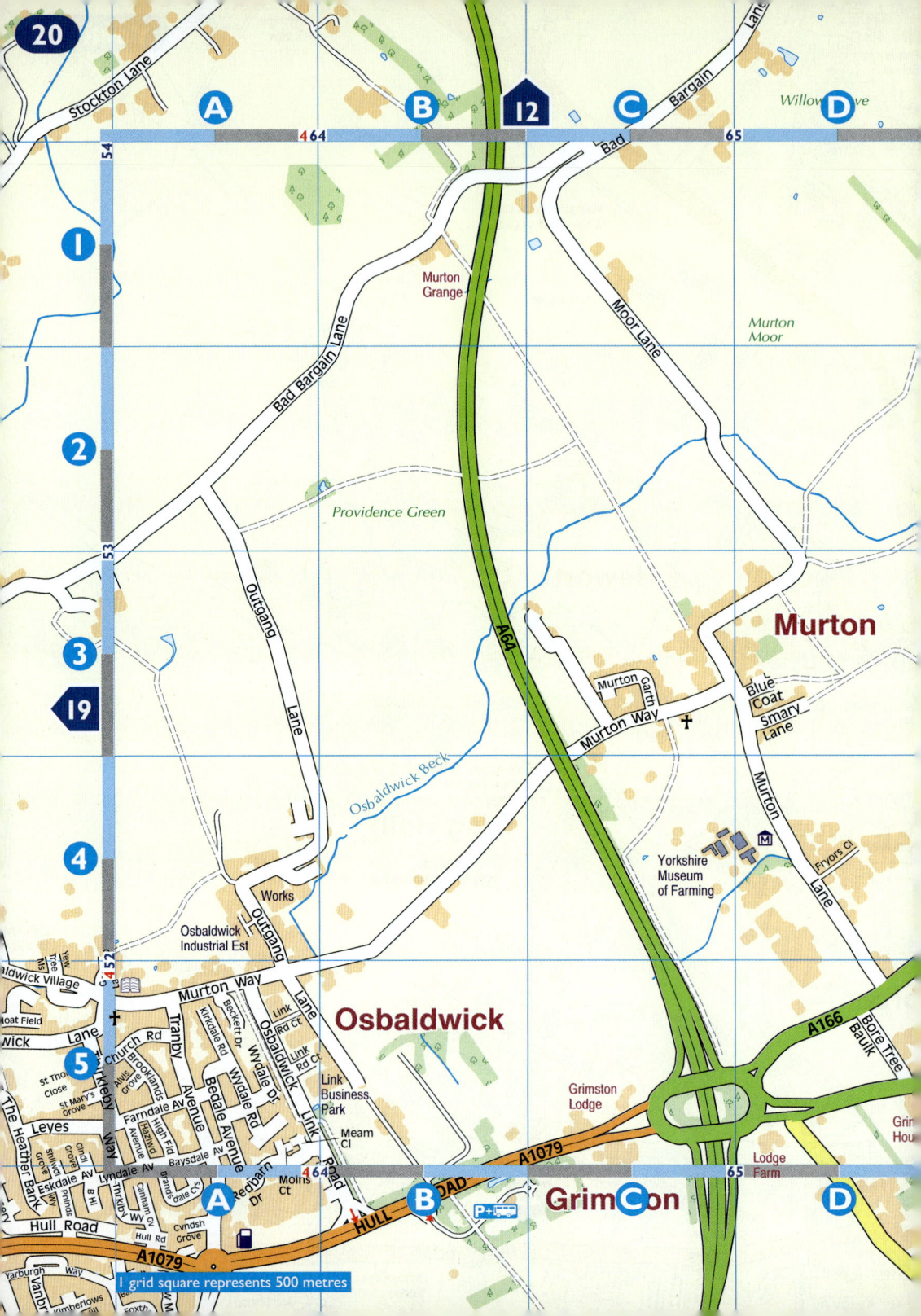

Osbaldwick Lane
Temple Avenue
Etty Avenue
Alcuin Avenue
Allen Cl
Flaxman Avenue
Tuke Avenue
Moore Av
Meadowbeck Cl
Hall Lane
19
E
F
G
H
Derwent Junior School
Broughton Way
Vicarage Gdns
Primary School
Leyes
St Thomas's Close
St Mary's Grove
Thirkleby Way
Church Rd
Brooklands
Alvis Grove
Farndale Av
High Fld
Hazlwd Avenue
Bedale Avenue
Lyndale Rd
Link Road
Link Business Park
Meam Cl
Moins Ct
Redbarn Dr
Baysdale Av
Wycliffe Av
Whitton Pl
Millfield Lane
Milson Gv
Owston Av
Lilac Avenue
Hadrian Av
Woolnough Avenue
Wolviston Av
Carlton Av
Sadberge Ct
Gardens
Nursery
Heather Bank
Eskdale Av
Lyndale Av
Thirkleby Wy
Cannam Gv
Brandsdale Cres
Cvndsh Grove
Hull Rd
Hull Road
HULL ROAD
A1079
HULL
Innkeeper's Lodge
Archbishop Holgates School
Yarburgh Way
Hesketh Bank
Low Mill Close
Vanbrugh Dr
Kimberlows Wood Hill
Foxthorn Pd
Deramore Dr
Deramore Drive West
Fernway
Sails Drive
Beaufort Close
Quant Ms
Windmill Lane
Newland Park Drive
Badger Hill Primary School
Bishopsway
Crossways
Brentwood Crs
Crescent
Badger Wood Walk
Field Lane
Sussex Road
Sussex Cl
Court
Eastfield Ct
Eastfield Crescent
Siwards How
Siwards Way
University of York
University Road
Hull & York Medical Sch
H Wy
Innovation Wy
Heslington
Lord Deramore's Primary School
School Lane
Enclsre Gdns
Hslngtn Ct
Btsn Cl
La Cl
Low Lane
Spring Lane
Walnut Cl
The Orch
Main St
Hall Pk
Holburns Cft
Street
James Wy
Goodricke Wy
Lane
Holmefield Lane
Peel Cl
Turner's Croft
W Moor La
Garroway Way
Manor House
YO10
Common Lane
Germany Beck
Golf Course
Grange Farm
Long Lane
A64
OX
Germany Lane
63
64
51
50
49
1
2
3
4
5
29
PO

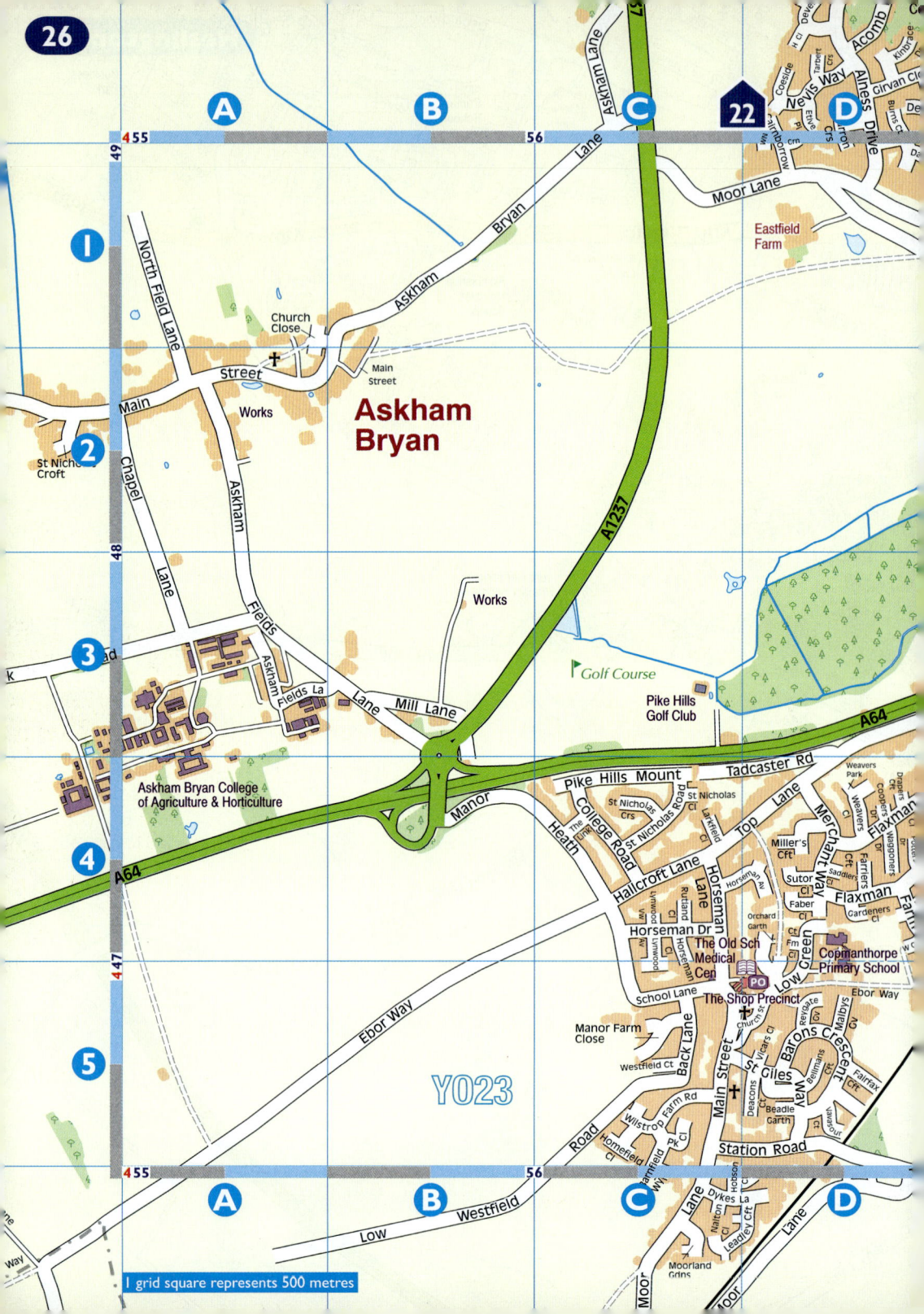

Askham Bryan

1 grid square represents 500 metres

Woodthorpe

Copmanthorpe 27

Middlethorpe

- Knavesmire Wood
- Manor Farm
- Middlethorpe Hall Hotel
- Middlethorpe Ings
- Hall Farm
- York City Crematorium
- River Ouse
- Ebor Way
- A64
- Bishopthorpe Road
- Trans Pennine Trail
- Green Lane
- Middlethorpe Grange

Bishopthorpe

- The Palace
- Riverside Caravan & Camping Park
- Bishopthorpe Infant School
- Junior School
- Church Lane
- Main Street
- Chantry Lane
- Ferry Lane
- Montague Rd
- Ramsey Avenue
- Myrtle Av
- Coda Av
- Acaster Lane
- Maple Avenue
- Beech Avenue
- Keble Park North
- Keble Park Crescent
- Keble Park South
- Sim Balk Lane
- Appleton Road
- Bridge Road
- York & Selby Path & Trans Pennine Trail
- Croft Croft
- Harcourt
- De Grey Pl
- Drummond
- Carbett Wy
- Lamplugh Crs
- Keble Dr
- Vernon Ct
- Wolsey Dr
- Melton Dr
- Neville Dr
- Beech Av
- Beech Ct
- Newlands Rd
- Deans
- Coplife
- The Coppice
- Copthorpe Lane
- Kirkwell
- New
- PO
- School
- McArthurGlen Designer Outlet Retail Park
- Naburn Lane
- B1222
- Works
- Acres House
- Naburn Lodge
- Naburn Marina
- Howden La
- River Ouse

1 grid square represents 500 metres

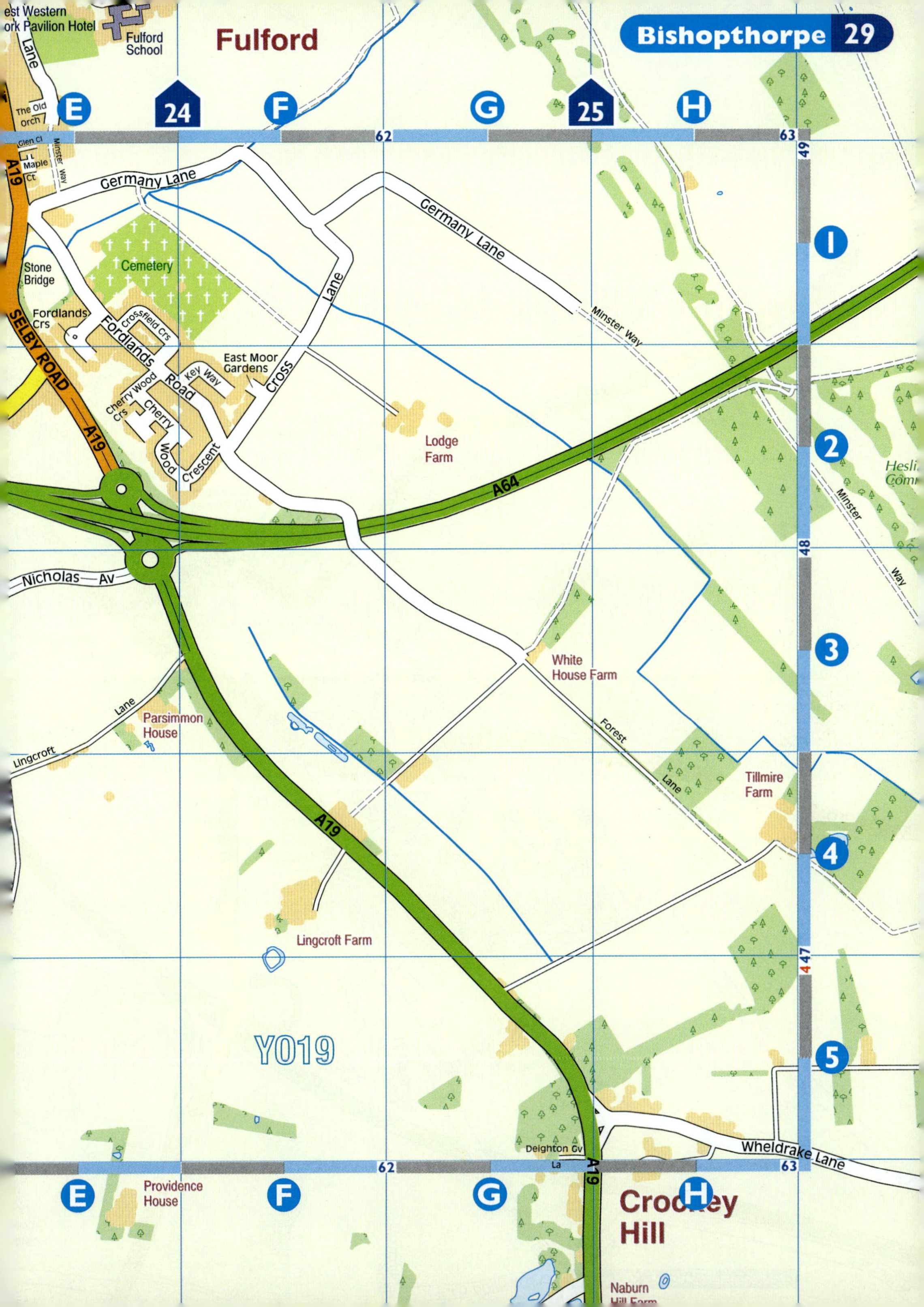

est Western
ork Pavilion Hotel
Fulford School
Fulford
Lane
The Old Orch
E
24
F
G
25
H
62
63
49
Glen Cl
Maple Ct
Minster Way
A19
Germany Lane
Germany Lane
Cemetery
Stone Bridge
Fordlands Crs
SELBY ROAD
Crossfield Crs
Fordlands Road
Key Way
East Moor Gardens
Cross Lane
Cherry Wood Crs
Cherry Wood Crescent
Minster Way
Lodge Farm
A64
I
2
Hesli Comm
Minster Way
48
3
Nicholas Av
White House Farm
Forest Lane
Lane
Lingcroft
Parsimmon House
Tillmire Farm
A19
4
Lingcroft Farm
47
5
YO19
Deighton Gv
La
Wheldrake Lane
62
63
E
F
G
H
Providence House
Crockey Hill
Naburn Hill Farm

A
B
C
D
1
2
3
4
5
447
48
44
43
442
TADCASTER
River Wharfe
A659
KELCBAR HILL
WETHERBY ROAD
Riverside Primary School
K Cl
Kelcbar Close
Kelcbar Way
Tower Crs
Smaws Farm
Westfield Ter
Westfield Crs
Westfield Sq
St Josephs RC Primary School
STATION RD
WESTGATE
KIRKGATE
PO
CHAPEL ST
St Joseph's St
Selby College
Tadcaster CC
Ind Est
HIGH STREET
BRIDGE ST
COMMERCIAL
Surg
Heatherdene
Wighill Lane
Ingleby Dr
Prospect Dr
Mill Lane
Rosemary Rw
Centre Lane
New St
Tadcaster Albion FC
Edgerton Garth
Edgerton Court
Edgerton Dr
Inholmes La
Edgerton Close
Station Road
Tadcaster Sports & Leisure Centre
Fairfield Road
Fairfield Way
F Rd
Aspen Wy
Cedar Dr
Beech Walk
Inholmes
LEEDS ROAD
Queen's Gdns
Magnet Sports Club
Tadcaster Ings
ROMAN ROAD
Cemetery
Dorchester Road
West Mt
Golf Links Crs
Golf Links Av
Golf Links Court
The Links
Stutton Road
Garnet Lane
Marlborough Av
Marlborough Drive
Willow
Sedge Rise
Broom Rd
Hillcrest Ct
Hillcrest Rise
C Crs
Calcaria Crs
Calcaria Rd
Woodlands
Wdl Vw
Windmill Grove
B R
Avenue
Firtree Crs
The Fairways
W Ri
Windmill Ri
Hawthorn Av
Hawthorn Croft
Hawthorn Close
A162
A64
Lane
Moor Lane
Stutton
Weedling Gate
Church Lane
Cork Beck
Grims Grang
1 grid square represents 500 metres

Tadcaster 31

Index – towns & villages

Acomb..................22 C2	Hall Garth..................21 G5	Middlethorpe..................28 B1	Stamford Bridge..................15 C
Askham Bryan..................26 B2	Haxby..................6 D3	Murton..................20 D3	Stockton on the Forest..................13 E
Bishopthorpe..................28 B4	Heslington..................25 E3	Nether Poppleton..................8 B4	Strensall..................5 H
Chapel Fields..................22 A1	Heworth..................19 F3	New Earswick..................10 D2	Tadcaster..................30 C
Clifton..................17 G2	Holgate..................23 F1	Nunthorpe..................23 H4	Tang Hall..................19 C
Copmanthorpe..................27 E4	Holtby..................13 H5	Osbaldwick..................20 B5	Walmgate Stray..................24 C
Dringhouses..................23 E4	Hopgrove..................12 A4	Overton..................8 A2	Warthill..................13 H
Dunnington..................21 G4	Huntington..................11 E3	Oxton..................31 G3	West Field..................22 A
Earswick..................7 G4	Knapton..................16 B4	Rawcliffe..................9 F4	Wigginton..................6 E
Fulford..................24 D5	Knavesmire..................23 G5	Skelton..................8 D2	Woodthorpe..................22 D
Gate Helmsley..................14 A2	Layerthorpe..................3 K4	South Bank..................23 G3	York..................2 E

USING THE STREET INDEX

Street names are listed alphabetically. Each street name is followed by its postal town or area locality, the Postcode District, the page number, and the reference to the square in which the name is found.

Standard index entries are shown as follows:

Abbey St *RAW/SKEL* YO30..................**17 H3**

Street names and selected addresses not shown on the map due to scale restrictions are shown in the index with an asterisk:

Albert St *FUL/HES* YO10 *..................**3 H6**

GENERAL ABBREVIATIONS

ACC..................ACCESS	E..................EAST	LDG..................LODGE	R..................RIVE
ALY..................ALLEY	EMB..................EMBANKMENT	LGT..................LIGHT	RBT..................ROUNDABOU
AP..................APPROACH	EMBY..................EMBASSY	LK..................LOCK	RD..................ROA
AR..................ARCADE	ESP..................ESPLANADE	LKS..................LAKES	RDG..................RIDC
ASS..................ASSOCIATION	EST..................ESTATE	LNDG..................LANDING	REP..................REPUBL
AV..................AVENUE	EX..................EXCHANGE	LTL..................LITTLE	RES..................RESERVO
BCH..................BEACH	EXPY..................EXPRESSWAY	LWR..................LOWER	RFC..................RUGBY FOOTBALL CLU
BLDS..................BUILDINGS	EXT..................EXTENSION	MAG..................MAGISTRATE	RI..................RIS
BND..................BEND	F/O..................FLYOVER	MAN..................MANSIONS	RP..................RAM
BNK..................BANK	FC..................FOOTBALL CLUB	MD..................MEAD	RW..................RO
BR..................BRIDGE	FK..................FORK	MDW..................MEADOWS	S..................SOU
BRK..................BROOK	FLD..................FIELD	MEM..................MEMORIAL	SCH..................SCHO
BTM..................BOTTOM	FLDS..................FIELDS	MI..................MILL	SE..................SOUTH EA
BUS..................BUSINESS	FLS..................FALLS	MKT..................MARKET	SER..................SERVICE ARE
BVD..................BOULEVARD	FM..................FARM	MKTS..................MARKETS	SH..................SHOR
BY..................BYPASS	FT..................FORT	ML..................MALL	SHOP..................SHOPPIN
CATH..................CATHEDRAL	FTS..................FLATS	MNR..................MANOR	SKWY..................SKYWA
CEM..................CEMETERY	FWY..................FREEWAY	MS..................MEWS	SMT..................SUMM
CEN..................CENTRE	FY..................FERRY	MSN..................MISSION	SOC..................SOCIE
CFT..................CROFT	GA..................GATE	MT..................MOUNT	SP..................SPU
CH..................CHURCH	GAL..................GALLERY	MTN..................MOUNTAIN	SPR..................SPRIN
CHA..................CHASE	GDN..................GARDEN	MTS..................MOUNTAINS	SQ..................SQUAR
CHYD..................CHURCHYARD	GDNS..................GARDENS	MUS..................MUSEUM	ST..................STREE
CIR..................CIRCLE	GLD..................GLADE	MWY..................MOTORWAY	STN..................STATIO
CIRC..................CIRCUS	GLN..................GLEN	N..................NORTH	STR..................STREA
CL..................CLOSE	GN..................GREEN	NE..................NORTH EAST	STRD..................STRAN
CLFS..................CLIFFS	GND..................GROUND	NW..................NORTH WEST	SW..................SOUTH WE
CMP..................CAMP	GRA..................GRANGE	O/P..................OVERPASS	TDG..................TRADIN
CNR..................CORNER	GRG..................GARAGE	OFF..................OFFICE	TER..................TERRAC
CO..................COUNTY	GT..................GREAT	ORCH..................ORCHARD	THWY..................THROUGHWA
COLL..................COLLEGE	GTWY..................GATEWAY	OV..................OVAL	TNL..................TUNN
COM..................COMMON	GV..................GROVE	PAL..................PALACE	TOLL..................TOLLW
COMM..................COMMISSION	HGR..................HIGHER	PAS..................PASSAGE	TPK..................TURNPI
CON..................CONVENT	HL..................HILL	PAV..................PAVILION	TR..................TRAC
COT..................COTTAGE	HLS..................HILLS	PDE..................PARADE	TRL..................TRA
COTS..................COTTAGES	HO..................HOUSE	PH..................PUBLIC HOUSE	TWR..................TOWE
CP..................CAPE	HOL..................HOLLOW	PK..................PARK	U/P..................UNDERPA
CPS..................COPSE	HOSP..................HOSPITAL	PKWY..................PARKWAY	UNI..................UNIVERSI
CR..................CREEK	HRB..................HARBOUR	PL..................PLACE	UPR..................UPP
CREM..................CREMATORIUM	HTH..................HEATH	PLN..................PLAIN	V..................VA
CRS..................CRESCENT	HTS..................HEIGHTS	PLNS..................PLAINS	VA..................VALL
CSWY..................CAUSEWAY	HVN..................HAVEN	PLZ..................PLAZA	VIAD..................VIADU
CT..................COURT	HWY..................HIGHWAY	POL..................POLICE STATION	VIL..................VIL
CTRL..................CENTRAL	IMP..................IMPERIAL	PR..................PRINCE	VIS..................VIS
CTS..................COURTS	IN..................INLET	PREC..................PRECINCT	VLG..................VILLA
CTYD..................COURTYARD	IND EST..................INDUSTRIAL ESTATE	PREP..................PREPARATORY	VLS..................VILL
CUTT..................CUTTINGS	INF..................INFIRMARY	PRIM..................PRIMARY	VW..................VIE
CV..................COVE	INFO..................INFORMATION	PROM..................PROMENADE	W..................WE
CYN..................CANYON	INT..................INTERCHANGE	PRS..................PRINCESS	WD..................WOO
DEPT..................DEPARTMENT	IS..................ISLAND	PRT..................PORT	WHF..................WHAR
DL..................DALE	JCT..................JUNCTION	PT..................POINT	WK..................WA
DM..................DAM	JTY..................JETTY	PTH..................PATH	WKS..................WAL
DR..................DRIVE	KG..................KING	PZ..................PIAZZA	WLS..................WEL
DRO..................DROVE	KNL..................KNOLL	QD..................QUADRANT	WY..................WA
DRY..................DRIVEWAY	L..................LAKE	QU..................QUEEN	YD..................YAR
DWGS..................DWELLINGS	LA..................LANE	QY..................QUAY	YHA..................YOUTH HOST

POSTCODE TOWNS AND AREA ABBREVIATIONS

ACOMB..................Acomb	CYK..................Central York	HXB/STR..................Haxby/Strensall	RYKW..................Rural York we
COP/BISH..................Copmanthorpe/Bishopthorpe	FUL/HES..................Fulford/Heslington	RAW/SKEL..................Rawcliffe/Skelton	STMFBR..................Stamford Brid
	HEWTH..................Heworth	RYKS..................Rural York south	TAD..................Tadcaster

Index - streets
Abb - Cal 33

A

bey St *RAW/SKEL* YO30 17 H3
botsford Rd *FUL/HES* YO10 24 D1
bot St *HEWTH* YO31 3 G1
botsway *HEWTH* YO31 18 D1
elton Gv *HXB/STR* YO32 6 D2
cacia Av *HXB/STR* YO32 10 D2
cacia Gv *HXB/STR* YO32 6 D2
caster La *COP/BISH* YO23 28 B5
comb Ct *ACOMB* YO24 * 22 D1
comb Ms *RYKW* YO26 22 C1
comb Rd *ACOMB* YO24 23 E1
comb Wood Cl *ACOMB* YO24 22 C5
comb Wood Dr *ACOMB* YO24 22 B5
corn Wy *ACOMB* YO24 22 D4
delaide St *COP/BISH* YO23 23 H2
dlington Cl *HXB/STR* YO32 5 F3
gar St *HEWTH* YO31 3 G2
nsty Av *ACOMB* YO24 23 F4
nsty Gv *ACOMB* YO24 23 F4
ntree Ct *ACOMB* YO24 23 F4
bany St *RYKW* YO26 17 G4
bemarle Rd *COP/BISH* YO23 23 H2
bert Cl *HEWTH* YO31 19 E1
bert St *FUL/HES* YO10 * 3 H6
bion Av *RYKW* YO26 16 C3
bion St *CYK* YO1 2 E6
cuin Av *FUL/HES* YO10 19 F5
cuin Wy *FUL/HES* YO10 25 F2
dborough Wy *RYKW* YO26 2 A3
derley Ct *HXB/STR* YO32 10 D3
dersyde *ACOMB* YO24 23 E5
der Wy *HXB/STR* YO32 10 C4
dreth Gv *COP/BISH* YO23 24 A2
dwark *CYK* YO1 3 G3
exander Av *HEWTH* YO31 10 D4
exandra Ct *FUL/HES* YO10 3 K5
exandra Rd *HXB/STR* YO32 5 F5
garth Ri *HEWTH* YO31 19 G2
garth Rd *HEWTH* YO31 19 G2
lan St *RAW/SKEL* YO30 18 B2
len Cl *FUL/HES* YO10 19 F5
lendale *ACOMB* YO24 22 D4
erton Dr *RYKW* YO26 8 A4
ington Dr *HEWTH* YO31 19 G3
ma Ct *FUL/HES* YO10 24 B2
ma Gv *FUL/HES* YO10 24 B2
ma Ter *FUL/HES* YO10 24 B2
mery Ter *RAW/SKEL* YO30 2 C3
mond Gv *HXB/STR* YO32 10 C2
nsford Dr *RYKW* YO26 16 C4
nsford Rd *RYKW* YO26 16 D4
ness Dr *ACOMB* YO24 22 B5
ne Ter *FUL/HES* YO10 24 C2
vis Gv *FUL/HES* YO10 20 A5
wyne Dr *RAW/SKEL* YO30 9 F5
wyne Gv *RAW/SKEL* YO30 9 F5
nberley St *RYKW* YO26 17 F4
nber St *HEWTH* YO31 18 C3
nbleside Av *FUL/HES* YO10 19 G5
nbrose St *FUL/HES* YO10 24 B3
ny Johnson Wy *RAW/SKEL* YO30 9 H3
cress Wk *COP/BISH* YO23 2 D7
croft Cl *CYK* YO1 3 G6
derson Gv *ACOMB* YO24 23 F2
drew Dr *HXB/STR* YO32 11 E5
gram Cl *RAW/SKEL* YO30 9 G5
nan Cl *ACOMB* YO24 27 E1
ne St *COP/BISH* YO23 24 A2
son Dr *FUL/HES* YO10 24 B4
thea Dr *HEWTH* YO31 10 D5
ollo Ct *FUL/HES* YO10 3 J7
ollo St *FUL/HES* YO10 3 J7
ple Blossom Ct *ACOMB* YO24 22 B3
pleby Gld *HXB/STR* YO32 6 D4
pleby Pl *HEWTH* YO31 19 F4
plecroft Rd *HEWTH* YO31 19 G2
ple Garth *RYKW* YO26 8 A5
pleton Ct *COP/BISH* YO23 27 H4
pleton Rd *COP/BISH* YO23 27 H4
enhall Cl *HXB/STR* YO32 6 C3
gyle St *COP/BISH* YO23 23 H3
lington Rd *RAW/SKEL* YO30 10 A5
mstrong Wy *RAW/SKEL* YO30 9 F3
ncliffe Ms *FUL/HES* YO10 * 24 B2
nside Pl *FUL/HES* YO10 24 D1
ran Pl *HEWTH* YO31 18 C2
thur Pl *RAW/SKEL* YO30 8 C1
thur St *FUL/HES* YO10 3 K6
undel Gv *ACOMB* YO24 22 C5
cot Rd *HXB/STR* YO32 6 B1
cot Wy *ACOMB* YO24 22 D2
hbourne Wy *ACOMB* YO24 22 C4
h Cl *HEWTH* YO31 19 G2
hdale Rd *RYKS* YO19 21 H4
Ashford Pl *ACOMB* YO24 22 D2
Ash La *HXB/STR* YO32 6 D1
Ashley Park Crs *HEWTH* YO31 19 G3
Ashley Park Rd *HEWTH* YO31 19 G2
Ashmeade Cl *ACOMB* YO24 22 B5
Ash St *RYKW* YO26 17 F5
Ashton Av *RAW/SKEL* YO30 18 B1
Ashville St *HEWTH* YO31 18 C2
Ash Wk *HXB/STR* YO32 5 G3
Ashwood Gld *HXB/STR* YO32 6 C5
Askham Bar *ACOMB* YO24 * 27 G1
Askham Bryan La *COP/BISH* YO23 26 C1
Askham Cft *ACOMB* YO24 22 B3
Askham Fields La *COP/BISH* YO23 26 B3
Askham Gv *ACOMB* YO24 22 B2
Askham La *COP/BISH* YO23 22 A5
Aspen Cl *RYKS* YO19 21 H3
Aspen Wy *TAD* LS24 30 B3
Asquith Av *HEWTH* YO31 19 F4
Atcherley Cl *FUL/HES* YO10 24 B4
Atlas Rd *RAW/SKEL* YO30 9 H3
Aucuba Cl *HXB/STR* YO32 10 C4
Audax Cl *RAW/SKEL* YO30 9 H3
Audax Rd *RAW/SKEL* YO30 9 H3
Auster Bank Av *TAD* LS24 31 E2
Auster Bank Crs *TAD* LS24 31 E2
Auster Bank Rd *TAD* LS24 31 E1
Auster Bank Vw *TAD* LS24 31 E1
Auster Rd *RAW/SKEL* YO30 9 H3
Avenue Rd *RAW/SKEL* YO30 18 A3
Avenue Ter *RAW/SKEL* YO30 18 A3
The Avenue *HXB/STR* YO32 6 C1
HXB/STR YO32 6 D3
RAW/SKEL YO30 2 B1
Aviator Ct *RAW/SKEL* YO30 9 G3
Avon Dr *HXB/STR* YO32 7 F5
Aylesham Ct *HXB/STR* YO32 10 D3

B

Bachelor Hl *ACOMB* YO24 22 C2
Backhouse St *HEWTH* YO31 3 F1
Back La *COP/BISH* YO23 26 C5
HXB/STR YO32 6 B2
RYKS YO19 21 G2
RYKW YO26 16 B4
Back Swinegate *CYK* YO1 3 F4
Back West Vw *RAW/SKEL* YO30 18 A2
Bad Bargain La *HEWTH* YO31 19 G3
RYKS YO19 12 C5
Badger Paddock *HEWTH* YO31 10 D4
Badger Wood Wk *FUL/HES* YO10 25 H2
Baildon Cl *RYKW* YO26 17 E5
Baile Hill Ter *CYK* YO1 2 E7
Baker St *RAW/SKEL* YO30 18 B2
Balfour St *RYKW* YO26 17 G4
Balfour Wy *HXB/STR* YO32 5 F4
Balmoral Ter *COP/BISH* YO23 23 H3
Bankside Cl *RYKW* YO26 8 A4
Bannisdale *ACOMB* YO24 22 C5
Barbara Gv *ACOMB* YO24 23 F1
Barbers Dr *COP/BISH* YO23 26 D4
Barbican Ms *FUL/HES* YO10 3 J6
Barbican Rd *FUL/HES* YO10 3 J7
Barden Ct *RAW/SKEL* YO30 9 G5
Barfield Rd *HEWTH* YO31 19 E1
Barker La *CYK* YO1 2 D5
Barkston Av *RYKW* YO26 22 A1
Barkston Cl *RYKW* YO26 22 A2
Barkston Gv *RYKW* YO26 22 A1
Barkston Rd *RYKW* YO26 22 A1
Bar La *CYK* YO1 2 C5
Barley Ri *HXB/STR* YO32 5 F4
Barley Vw *HXB/STR* YO32 6 C3
Barlow St *RYKW* YO26 17 E5
Barmby Av *FUL/HES* YO10 24 C4
Barmby Cl *RAW/SKEL* YO30 9 G5
Barons Crs *COP/BISH* YO23 26 D5
Barrett Av *ACOMB* YO24 23 F1
Barstow Av *FUL/HES* YO10 24 D1
Bartle Garth *CYK* YO1 * 3 G3
Barton Cl *RAW/SKEL* YO30 9 F4
Bateson Cl *FUL/HES* YO10 25 G3
Battleflats Wy *STMFBR* YO41 15 G3
Baysdale Av *FUL/HES* YO10 25 H1
Beaconsfield Ms *ACOMB* YO24 22 D1
Beaconsfield St *ACOMB* YO24 22 D1
Beadle Garth *COP/BISH* YO23 26 D5
Beagle Cft *STMFBR* YO41 15 E4
Beagle Ridge Dr *ACOMB* YO24 22 C3
Beagle Spinney *STMFBR* YO41 15 E4
Beanland La *HXB/STR* YO32 13 E2
Bean's Wy *HEWTH* YO31 19 G1
Beaufort Cl *FUL/HES* YO10 25 F1
Beaulieu Cl *HXB/STR* YO32 11 E1
Beaverdyke *RAW/SKEL* YO30 9 G5
Beckett Dr *FUL/HES* YO10 20 A5
Beckfield La *RYKW* YO26 16 C5
Beckfield Pl *RYKW* YO26 16 C5
Beckside Gdns *FUL/HES* YO10 19 E5
Beckwith Cl *HEWTH* YO31 19 H2
Bedale Av *FUL/HES* YO10 20 A5
Bede Av *RAW/SKEL* YO30 18 A2
Bedern *CYK* YO1 * 3 G3
Beech Av *ACOMB* YO24 23 F1
COP/BISH YO23 28 A4
Beech Cl *TAD* LS24 31 E3
Beech Ct *COP/BISH* YO23 28 A4
The Beeches *RAW/SKEL* YO30 8 D1
RYKW YO26 8 A4
Beech Gld *HEWTH* YO31 11 E4
Beech Gv *RYKW* YO26 16 D5
Beech Pl *HXB/STR* YO32 5 F4
Beechtree Rd *TAD* LS24 30 B4
Beech Wk *TAD* LS24 30 B3
Beech Wy *RYKW* YO26 8 A5
Beechwood Gld *ACOMB* YO24 22 B3
Beeforth Cl *HXB/STR* YO32 10 C1
Belcombe Wy *RAW/SKEL* YO30 17 H2
Belgrave St *HEWTH* YO31 18 B2
Bell Cl *HXB/STR* YO32 6 C3
Belle Vue St *FUL/HES* YO10 3 J7
Belle Vue Ter *FUL/HES* YO10 3 K7
Bellfarm Av *HEWTH* YO31 18 D1
Bellhouse Wy *ACOMB* YO24 22 C3
Bellmans Cft *COP/BISH* YO23 26 D5
Bellwood Dr *ACOMB* YO24 22 B4
Belmont Cl *RAW/SKEL* YO30 9 G5
Beresford Ter *COP/BISH* YO23 24 A3
Berkeley Ter *RYKW* YO26 17 F4
Beverley Balk *STMFBR* YO41 14 B3
Beverley Gdns *HEWTH* YO31 * 3 J1
Bewlay St *COP/BISH* YO23 24 A2
Bilsdale Cl *RAW/SKEL* YO30 9 F4
Birch La *HXB/STR* YO32 6 D2
Birch Pk *HEWTH* YO31 10 D5
Birch Tree Cl *HXB/STR* YO32 5 F4
Birkdale Gv *RYKW* YO26 16 C4
Birstwith Dr *RYKW* YO26 17 F5
Bishopgate St *COP/BISH* YO23 2 E7
Bishophill Junior *CYK* YO1 2 E6
Bishophill Senior *CYK* YO1 2 E6
Bishops Ct *CYK* YO1 * 2 E6
Bishopsfileds Dr *RYKW* YO26 2 A4
Bishopsway *FUL/HES* YO10 25 G1
Bishopthorpe Rd *COP/BISH* YO23 28 B3
Bismarck St *RYKW* YO26 17 G4
Black Dike La *RYKW* YO26 16 A1
Blacklee Cl *HXB/STR* YO32 5 H1
Blackthorn Dr *HEWTH* YO31 10 D4
Blakeley Gv *RAW/SKEL* YO30 9 G3
Blakeney Pl *FUL/HES* YO10 3 K7
Blake St *CYK* YO1 2 E3
Bland La *RYKW* YO26 16 B5
Blatchford Ct *RAW/SKEL* YO30 10 A5
Blenheim Ct *RAW/SKEL* YO30 9 E3
Bleriot Wy *RAW/SKEL* YO30 9 H3
Blossom St *ACOMB* YO24 2 C6
Blue Beck Dr *RAW/SKEL* YO30 17 F1
Blue Bridge La *FUL/HES* YO10 24 B2
Blue Coat *RYKS* YO19 20 D3
Board St *COP/BISH* YO23 24 A2
Bog La *ACOMB* YO24 26 D1
Bollans Ct *CYK* YO1 * 3 G3
Boltby Rd *RAW/SKEL* YO30 9 G4
Bonington Ct *RYKW* YO26 17 F4
Bootham *RAW/SKEL* YO30 2 D2
Bootham Crs *RAW/SKEL* YO30 2 D1
Bootham Park Ct *HEWTH* YO31 * 18 B3
Bootham Rw *RAW/SKEL* YO30 2 E2
Bootham Sq *RAW/SKEL* YO30 2 E2
Bootham Ter *RAW/SKEL* YO30 2 C2
Boothwood Rd *RAW/SKEL* YO30 9 G4
Bore Tree Baulk *RYKS* YO19 20 D5
Boroughbridge Rd *RYKW* YO26 16 D3
Borrowdale Dr *RAW/SKEL* YO30 9 G5
Bouthwaite Dr *RYKW* YO26 17 F5
Bow Bridge Vw *TAD* LS24 31 F1
Bowes Av *HEWTH* YO31 3 K3
Bowland Wy *RAW/SKEL* YO30 9 H5
Bowling Green Cft *HEWTH* YO31 18 C1
Bowling Green La *HEWTH* YO31 3 G1
Bowness Dr *RAW/SKEL* YO30 9 F5
Bowyers Cl *COP/BISH* YO23 27 E4
Bracken Cl *HXB/STR* YO32 11 E2
Bracken Hl *FUL/HES* YO10 25 G1
Brackenhills *RYKW* YO26 8 A5
Bracken Rd *ACOMB* YO24 23 F5
Bradley Dr *ACOMB* YO24 22 C4
Braeside Gdns *ACOMB* YO24 17 F5
Brailsford Crs *RAW/SKEL* YO30 17 H1
Bramble Dene *ACOMB* YO24 22 D5
Bramham Av *RYKW* YO26 22 A1
Bramham Gv *RYKW* YO26 22 A1
Bramham Rd *RYKW* YO26 22 A2
Bramley Garth *HEWTH* YO31 19 G3
Brandon Gv *HXB/STR* YO32 12 B3
Brandsby Gv *HEWTH* YO31 10 D4
Brandsdale Crs *FUL/HES* YO10 25 H1
Bransholme Dr *RAW/SKEL* YO30 9 H4
Branton Pl *RYKW* YO26 22 A1
Bray Rd *FUL/HES* YO10 24 D4
Breary Cl *ACOMB* YO24 23 F3
Brecks Cl *HXB/STR* YO32 6 C3
Brecksfield *RAW/SKEL* YO30 8 D1
Brecks La *HXB/STR* YO32 5 H2
HXB/STR YO32 11 E2
Brentwood Crs *FUL/HES* YO10 25 G2
Bretgate *CYK* YO1 * 3 J6
Briar Av *RYKW* YO26 16 C5
Briar Dr *HEWTH* YO31 11 E5
Bridge Cl *HXB/STR* YO32 6 C4
Bridge Rd *COP/BISH* YO23 27 H4
Bridge St *CYK* YO1 2 E5
TAD LS24 30 D3
Bridle Wy *RYKW* YO26 22 A1
Bridlington Rd *STMFBR* YO41 15 G2
Briergate *HXB/STR* YO32 6 D4
Briggs St *HEWTH* YO31 18 B2
Bright St *RYKW* YO26 17 G4
Brinkworth Ter *FUL/HES* YO10 3 J6
Broad Acres *HXB/STR* YO32 6 C4
Broad La *COP/BISH* YO23 22 A2
Broad Oak La *HXB/STR* YO32 6 C2
Broadstone Wy *RAW/SKEL* YO30 9 F3
Broadway *FUL/HES* YO10 24 B4
Broadway Gv *FUL/HES* YO10 24 C4
Broadway West *FUL/HES* YO10 24 B4
Brockfield Park Dr *HEWTH* YO31 10 D4
Brockfield Rd *HEWTH* YO31 10 D4
Bromley St *RYKW* YO26 17 G4
Brompton Rd *RAW/SKEL* YO30 17 H2
Brooklands *FUL/HES* YO10 20 A5
Brook St *HEWTH* YO31 3 F1
Broome Cl *HXB/STR* YO32 11 E1
Broome Rd *HXB/STR* YO32 11 F1
Broome Wy *HXB/STR* YO32 11 F1
Broom Rd *TAD* LS24 30 B4
Brougham Cl *RAW/SKEL* YO30 17 G1
Broughton Wy *FUL/HES* YO10 19 G5
Browney Cft *FUL/HES* YO10 3 G7
Brownlow St *HEWTH* YO31 3 G1
Brown Moor *STMFBR* YO41 15 G3
Brunel Ct *RYKW* YO26 17 G4
Brunswick St *COP/BISH* YO23 23 H3
Buckingham Ct *CYK* YO1 * 2 D6
Buckingham St *CYK* YO1 2 E6
Buckingham Ter *CYK* YO1 * 2 E6
Bull La *FUL/HES* YO10 24 D1
HEWTH YO31 19 E3
Burdyke Av *RAW/SKEL* YO30 17 H1
Burlington Av *FUL/HES* YO10 19 E5
Burnholme Av *HEWTH* YO31 19 G3
Burnholme Dr *HEWTH* YO31 19 F3
Burnholme Gv *HEWTH* YO31 19 F4
Burniston Gv *FUL/HES* YO10 19 F5
Burnsall Dr *RYKW* YO26 17 F5
Burns Ct *ACOMB* YO24 22 B5
Burrill Av *RAW/SKEL* YO30 18 A1
Burrill Dr *HXB/STR* YO32 6 B2
Burton Av *RAW/SKEL* YO30 18 A2
Burton Fields Rd *STMFBR* YO41 15 G2
Burton Gn *RAW/SKEL* YO30 18 A1
Burton Stone La *RAW/SKEL* YO30 18 A3
Burtree Av *RAW/SKEL* YO30 8 C2
Butcher Ter *COP/BISH* YO23 24 A3
Buttercrambe Rd *STMFBR* YO41 15 E1
Buttermere Dr *RAW/SKEL* YO30 9 F5
Butters Cl *HXB/STR* YO32 6 B2
Butt Hl *HXB/STR* YO32 6 B2
Butts Cl *STMFBR* YO41 15 F4
Byland Av *HEWTH* YO31 18 D1
Byron Dr *RAW/SKEL* YO30 17 G1

C

Caedmon Cl *HEWTH* YO31 19 F2
Caesar Ct *COP/BISH* YO23 2 D7
Cairnborrow *ACOMB* YO24 22 B5
Caithness Cl *RAW/SKEL* YO30 9 F3
Calcaria Ct *ACOMB* YO24 23 F4
Calcaria Crs *TAD* LS24 30 B4
Calcaria Rd *TAD* LS24 30 B4
Caldbeck Cl *RAW/SKEL* YO30 9 H5

34 Cal - Ell

Calder Av *RYKW* YO26 16 C1
Calf Cl *HXB/STR* YO32 6 D3
Calvert Cl *HXB/STR* YO32 6 C4
Cambrian Cl *HXB/STR* YO32 11 E3
Cambridge Ms *ACOMB* YO24 * 2 B6
Cambridge St *ACOMB* YO24 2 B6
Cameron Gv *COP/BISH* YO23 24 A3
Cameron Walker Ct
COP/BISH YO23 * 24 A2
Campbell Av *ACOMB* YO24 23 E2
Campleshon Rd
COP/BISH YO23 23 H3
Canham Gv *FUL/HES* YO10 25 H1
Canterbury Cl *HXB/STR* YO32 6 B1
Carey St *FUL/HES* YO10 24 B3
Carleton St *RYKW* YO26 17 G4
Carlisle St *RYKW* YO26 17 G4
Carl St *COP/BISH* YO23 24 A2
Carlton Av *FUL/HES* YO10 25 F1
Carmelite St *CYK* YO1 3 G4
Carmires Av *HXB/STR* YO32 7 E2
Carnot St *RYKW* YO26 17 G4
Carnoustie Cl *RYKW* YO26 16 C5
Caroline Cl *ACOMB* YO24 23 F1
Carrbank La *RYKS* YO19 13 F2
Carrfield *ACOMB* YO24 22 C4
Carrick Gdns *ACOMB* YO24 23 E1
Carrington Av *RYKW* YO26 17 F4
Carr La *RYKW* YO26 17 E5
Carrnock Ct *HXB/STR* YO32 11 E5
Carron Crs *ACOMB* YO24 22 B5
Carter Av *HEWTH* YO31 19 E4
Castle Cl *HXB/STR* YO32 6 A1
Castlegate *CYK* YO1 3 F5
Catherine Ct *FUL/HES* YO10 3 K6
Catterton La *TAD* LS24 31 H1
Cavendish Gv *FUL/HES* YO10 25 H1
Caxton Av *RYKW* YO26 17 E4
Cayley Cl *RAW/SKEL* YO30 9 G5
Cayley Ct *RAW/SKEL* YO30 * 9 H4
Cecelia Pl *ACOMB* YO24 2 A6
Cecilia Pl *ACOMB* YO24 * 2 A6
Cedar Dr *TAD* LS24 30 B3
Cedar Gld *RYKS* YO19 21 G4
Cedar Gv *HEWTH* YO31 19 G2
Cedarwood Cl *ACOMB* YO24 22 B3
Celtic Cl *RYKW* YO26 16 C4
Cemetery Rd *FUL/HES* YO10 24 B2
Centenary Wy *CYK* YO1 3 F2
HXB/STR YO32 7 F5
HXB/STR YO32 11 E1
Centre La *TAD* LS24 30 D3
Centurion Wy *RAW/SKEL* YO30 10 A3
Chaldon Cl *HXB/STR* YO32 5 F4
Chalfonts *ACOMB* YO24 23 F3
Chaloner's Crs *ACOMB* YO24 22 D5
Chaloner's Rd *ACOMB* YO24 22 D4
Chancery Ct *ACOMB* YO24 22 C1
Chancery Ri *ACOMB* YO24 23 F1
Chantry Cl *ACOMB* YO24 22 C5
Chantry Gap *RYKW* YO26 8 A5
Chantry Gv *RYKW* YO26 8 A5
Chantry La *COP/BISH* YO23 28 B3
Chapel Fields Rd *RYKW* YO26 22 B1
Chapel Rw *CYK* YO1 3 H6
Chapel St *TAD* LS24 30 C3
Chapmans Ct *ACOMB* YO24 27 F1
Chapter House St *CYK* YO1 3 F3
Charles Moor *HEWTH* YO31 19 E2
Charlotte St *FUL/HES* YO10 3 K5
Charlton St *COP/BISH* YO23 24 A2
Chase Side Ct *ACOMB* YO24 23 E4
Chatsworth Av *HXB/STR* YO32 5 H1
Chatsworth Dr *HXB/STR* YO32 7 F2
Chatsworth Ter *RYKW* YO26 17 F5
Chaucer La *HXB/STR* YO32 5 H1
Chaucer St *FUL/HES* YO10 3 K6
Chaumont Wy *HXB/STR* YO32 12 D2
Chelkar Wy *RAW/SKEL* YO30 9 G5
Chelwood Wk *RYKW* YO26 17 F5
Cherry Garth *HEWTH* YO31 19 G4
Cherry Gv *RYKW* YO26 8 A5
Cherry Hill La *COP/BISH* YO23 * 3 F7
Cherry La *ACOMB* YO24 23 F4
Cherry Orch *HXB/STR* YO32 * 6 D3
Cherry Paddock *HXB/STR* YO32 6 D3
STMFBR YO41 15 E3
Cherry St *COP/BISH* YO23 3 F7
Cherry Tree Av *HXB/STR* YO32 10 C2
Cherry Wood Crs *RYKS* YO19 29 F2
Cheshire Av *HXB/STR* YO32 5 F5
Cheshire Cl *RAW/SKEL* YO30 9 F4
Chesney Flds *ACOMB* YO24 22 D3
Chessingham Gdns
ACOMB YO24 27 G1
Chessingham Pk *RYKS* YO19 21 H5
Chestnut Av *HEWTH* YO31 19 E2
Chestnut Gv *RYKW* YO26 16 D5
The Chestnuts *HXB/STR* YO32 6 C3
Cheviot Cl *HXB/STR* YO32 11 E3
Chiltern Wy *HXB/STR* YO32 11 E1
Chipstead Wk *HXB/STR* YO32 5 F3
Chudleigh Rd *RYKW* YO26 17 G4
Church Balk *RYKS* YO19 21 G3
Church Cl *COP/BISH* YO23 26 A1
Churchfield Dr *HXB/STR* YO32 6 C2
Church La *COP/BISH* YO23 28 A3
CYK YO1 3 F5
HXB/STR YO32 5 F2
HXB/STR YO32 6 C2
HXB/STR YO32 10 D1
RAW/SKEL YO30 8 C1
RYKS YO19 21 G3
RYKW YO26 8 B4
STMFBR YO41 15 F3
Church Ms *RYKW* YO26 22 C1
Church Ri *RYKS* YO19 13 H5
Church Rd *FUL/HES* YO10 19 H5
STMFBR YO41 15 F3
Church St *COP/BISH* YO23 26 C5
CYK YO1 3 F4
RYKS YO19 21 G3
Cinder La *ACOMB* YO24 2 B5
HEWTH YO31 3 K1
RYKW YO26 16 B2
RYKW YO26 17 G4
Cinder Ms *RYKW* YO26 2 A2
City Mills *CYK* YO1 * 3 F6
Claremont Ter *HEWTH* YO31 2 E1
Clarence St *HEWTH* YO31 3 F1
Clarks Ter *HEWTH* YO31 * 19 E3
Claygate *HEWTH* YO31 19 G3
Clay Pl *ACOMB* YO24 22 D3
Clementhorpe *COP/BISH* YO23 2 E7
Clement St *COP/BISH* YO23 2 E7
Cleveland St *ACOMB* YO24 2 A5
Cleveland Wy *HXB/STR* YO32 11 E3
Clifford St *CYK* YO1 3 F5
Clifton Dl *RAW/SKEL* YO30 17 H3
Clifton Gn *RAW/SKEL* YO30 17 H2
Clifton Moor Ga *RAW/SKEL* YO30 9 H4
Clifton Park Av *RAW/SKEL* YO30 17 F1
Clifton Pl *RAW/SKEL* YO30 17 H2
Clifton Rd *RAW/SKEL* YO30 17 H3
Clive Gv *ACOMB* YO24 23 F2
The Cloisters *HEWTH* YO31 3 G2
Cloisters Wk *HEWTH* YO31 3 G3
Cloister Wk *HEWTH* YO31 * 3 G3
The Close *RAW/SKEL* YO30 17 G1
Cloverley Cl *STMFBR* YO41 15 E3
Cobble Court Ms *ACOMB* YO24 * 2 C7
Cobham Wy *RAW/SKEL* YO30 9 F4
Coda Av *COP/BISH* YO23 28 B4
Coeside *ACOMB* YO24 22 B5
Coggan Cl *COP/BISH* YO23 * 23 H2
Coggan Wy *COP/BISH* YO23 27 H3
Coledale Cl *RAW/SKEL* YO30 9 G5
Colenso St *COP/BISH* YO23 3 F7
Cole St *HEWTH* YO31 3 F1
Colliergate *CYK* YO1 3 F4
College Rd *COP/BISH* YO23 26 C4
College St *CYK* YO1 3 F3
Collingham Pl *RYKW* YO26 * 16 C5
Collingwood Av *ACOMB* YO24 23 F2
Coltons Cottages
RAW/SKEL YO30 * 18 A2
Commercial St *TAD* LS24 30 D3
Common La *FUL/HES* YO10 25 G4
Common Rd *RYKS* YO19 21 H4
Compton St *RAW/SKEL* YO30 17 H3
Concorde Pk *RAW/SKEL* YO30 9 H3
Coneycroft *RYKS* YO19 21 H3
Coney St *CYK* YO1 2 E4
Conifer Cl *HXB/STR* YO32 10 C4
Coningham Av *RAW/SKEL* YO30 9 F4
Coniston Cl *RAW/SKEL* YO30 9 F5
Coniston Dr *FUL/HES* YO10 19 G5
Connaught Ct *FUL/HES* YO10 * 24 B4
Connaught Wy *HXB/STR* YO32 7 F5
Constantine Av *FUL/HES* YO10 19 F5
Conway Cl *RAW/SKEL* YO30 9 F3
Coopers Dr *COP/BISH* YO23 26 D4
Copmanthorpe La
COP/BISH YO23 27 H4
Copperbeech Cl *RYKS* YO19 21 G3
The Copper Beeches
RYKS YO19 21 G3
Coppergate *CYK* YO1 3 F5
Coppergate Wk *CYK* YO1 * 3 F5
Coppice Cl *HXB/STR* YO32 6 D1
The Coppice *COP/BISH* YO23 27 H3
Copwood Gv *HXB/STR* YO32 6 C3
Corban Wy *HXB/STR* YO32 6 B2
Corlett Ct *ACOMB* YO24 22 C4
Cornborough Av *HEWTH* YO31 19 E3
Corncroft *HXB/STR* YO32 5 F4
Corner Cl *HXB/STR* YO32 6 A2
Cornlands Rd *ACOMB* YO24 22 C2
Cornwall Dr *FUL/HES* YO10 24 C4
Cornwood Wy *HXB/STR* YO32 6 C3
Cosmo Av *HEWTH* YO31 19 E4
Cotswold Wy *HXB/STR* YO32 11 F1
Cottage Ms *HEWTH* YO31 * 19 F3
Count De Burgh Ter
COP/BISH YO23 23 H3
Courcey Gv *RYKW* YO26 16 D5
The Courtyard *COP/BISH* YO23 28 B3
The Covert *ACOMB* YO24 23 F5
Coxlea Gv *HEWTH* YO31 19 G3
Crabtree Gv *HXB/STR* YO32 10 C3
Cranbrook Av *RYKW* YO26 16 D4
Cranbrook Rd *RYKW* YO26 16 D3
Cranfield Pl *ACOMB* YO24 22 C4
Crawley Wy *HEWTH* YO31 19 G3
Creaser Cl *HXB/STR* YO32 5 F3
The Crescent *ACOMB* YO24 2 C6
STMFBR YO41 15 F3
Crichton Av *RAW/SKEL* YO30 18 B2
Crinan Ct *HXB/STR* YO32 7 F5
Croft Ct *COP/BISH* YO23 28 A3
Croft Farm Cl *COP/BISH* YO23 26 D4
Croftside *RYKW* YO26 22 B1
The Croft *HXB/STR* YO32 5 G4
Croftway *RYKW* YO26 22 B1
Crombie Av *RAW/SKEL* YO30 18 A2
Cromer St *RAW/SKEL* YO30 18 A2
Cromwell Rd *CYK* YO1 2 E6
Crookland La *HXB/STR* YO32 6 D1
Crossfield Crs *RYKS* YO19 29 E1
Crosslands Rd *FUL/HES* YO10 24 C4
Cross La *RYKS* YO19 29 F2
Crossmoor La *HXB/STR* YO32 4 B4
Cross St *ACOMB* YO24 22 C1
Crossways *FUL/HES* YO10 25 G2
The Crossway *HEWTH* YO31 18 D1
Crummock *ACOMB* YO24 22 C5
Cumberland Cl *HXB/STR* YO32 5 G4
Cumberland St *CYK* YO1 3 F5
Cumbrian Av *HXB/STR* YO32 5 G4
Curlew Glebe *RYKS* YO19 21 G4
Curzon Ter *COP/BISH* YO23 23 H3
Custance Wk *COP/BISH* YO23 2 D7
Cycle St *FUL/HES* YO10 25 E1
Cygnet St *COP/BISH* YO23 2 D7
Cyprus Gv *HXB/STR* YO32 6 D1

D

Dalby Md *HEWTH* YO31 11 E5
Dale Dike Gv *RAW/SKEL* YO30 9 G4
Dale's La *HEWTH* YO31 19 E3
Dale St *COP/BISH* YO23 2 D7
Dalguise Gv *HEWTH* YO31 3 H1
Dalmally Cl *ACOMB* YO24 26 D1
Dalton Ter *ACOMB* YO24 2 B7
Dane Av *RYKW* YO26 16 D5
Danebury Crs *RYKW* YO26 16 D5
Danebury Dr *RYKW* YO26 16 D5
Danes Cft *FUL/HES* YO10 * 24 B4
Danesfort Av *ACOMB* YO24 22 D2
Danesgate *RYKW* YO26 16 D5
Danesmead *FUL/HES* YO10 24 B4
Daneswell Cl *STMFBR* YO41 15 G2
Danum Dr *FUL/HES* YO10 24 C4
Danum Rd *FUL/HES* YO10 24 C4
Darbie Cl *HXB/STR* YO32 10 C2
Darfield Cl *HXB/STR* YO32 5 H1
Darley Cl *STMFBR* YO41 15 G2
Darnborough St
COP/BISH YO23 2 E7
Darnbrook Wk *HEWTH* YO31 19 G4
Darwin Cl *HEWTH* YO31 10 D5
Davygate *CYK* YO1 2 E4
Daysfoot Ct *FUL/HES* YO10 3 K7
Deacons Ct *COP/BISH* YO23 26 D5
Dealtry Av *HXB/STR* YO32 6 C3
Deangate *CYK* YO1 3 F3
Deanhead Gv *RAW/SKEL* YO30 9 F4
Deans Cl *COP/BISH* YO23 27 H3
Dee Cl *ACOMB* YO24 22 B5
Deepdale *ACOMB* YO24 22 D4
Deer Hill Gv *RAW/SKEL* YO30 9 G3
Deerstone Wy *RYKS* YO19 21 H4
De Grey Ct *RAW/SKEL* YO30 18 A3
De Grey Pl *COP/BISH* YO23 28 B4
De Grey St *HEWTH* YO31 3 F1
De Grey Ter *HEWTH* YO31 3 F1
Deighton Grove La *RYKS* YO19 29 G5
Delamere Cl *HXB/STR* YO32 6 B1
The Dell *RAW/SKEL* YO30 8 C1
Del Pyke *HEWTH* YO31 3 F1
Delwood *FUL/HES* YO10 24 B5
Dennison St *HEWTH* YO31 3 H1
Dennis St *CYK* YO1 3 G5
Deramore Dr *FUL/HES* YO10 25 H1
Deramore Dr West
FUL/HES YO10 25 C
Derwent Av *FUL/HES* YO10 19 E
Derwent Cl *STMFBR* YO41 15 C
Derwent Est *RYKS* YO19 21 F
Derwent La *RYKS* YO19 21 C
Derwent Rd *FUL/HES* YO10 24 E
Deveron Wy *ACOMB* YO24 22 E
Devon Pl *FUL/HES* YO10 24 D
Devonshire Ct *RAW/SKEL* YO30 9 H
Dewsbury Cottages
ACOMB YO24 2 D
Dewsbury Ter *CYK* YO1 2 D
Diamond St *HEWTH* YO31 18 C
Dickens Cl *HXB/STR* YO32 18 C
Dickson Rd *ACOMB* YO24 22 B
Didsbury Cl *RAW/SKEL* YO30 9 F
Dijon Av *ACOMB* YO24 22 C
Dikelands Cl *RYKW* YO26 8 A
Dikelands La *RYKW* YO26 8 A
Dilys Gv *RYKW* YO26 17 F
Disraeli Cl *HXB/STR* YO32 10 C
Dixon La *CYK* YO1 3 C
Dodgson Ter *RYKW* YO26 17 E
Dodsworth Av *HEWTH* YO31 18 D
Doe Pk *RAW/SKEL* YO30 9 C
Don Av *ACOMB* YO24 23 E
Dorchester Rd *TAD* LS24 30 E
Doriam Av *HEWTH* YO31 11 E
Doriam Dr *HEWTH* YO31 10 D
Dove St *COP/BISH* YO23 2 D
Drakes Cl *HXB/STR* YO32 11
Drake St *COP/BISH* YO23 2 E
Drapers Cft *COP/BISH* YO23 26 D
Driffield Ter *ACOMB* YO24 23 C
Dringfield Cl *ACOMB* YO24 22 D
Dringthorpe Rd *ACOMB* YO24 23
Drome Rd *COP/BISH* YO23 27
Drummond Vw *COP/BISH* YO23 28 E
Dudley Ct *HEWTH* YO31 3 C
Dudley Ms *HEWTH* YO31 18 C
Dudley St *HEWTH* YO31 18 C
Dukes Ct *RYKW* YO26 17
Dukes Whf *COP/BISH* YO23 * 3
Duncombe Dr *HXB/STR* YO32 5 F
Duncombe Pl *CYK* YO1 2
Dundas St *CYK* YO1 3 C
Durlston Dr *HXB/STR* YO32 5

E

Eades Cl *RAW/SKEL* YO30 17
Earle St *HEWTH* YO31 18
Earlsborough Ter
RAW/SKEL YO30 * 2
Earswick Cha *HXB/STR* YO32 7
Earswick Village *HXB/STR* YO32 7
Eason Rd *ACOMB* YO24 23
Eason Vw *ACOMB* YO24 23
Eastbourne Gv *HEWTH* YO31 19
East Cottages
RAW/SKEL YO30 * 17
Eastern Ter *HEWTH* YO31 3
Eastfield Av *HXB/STR* YO32 6
Eastfield Cl *TAD* LS24 31
Eastfield Ct *FUL/HES* YO10 25
Eastfield Crs *FUL/HES* YO10 25
Eastholme Dr *RAW/SKEL* YO30 9
Easthorpe Dr *RYKW* YO26 8
East Moor Gdns *RYKS* YO19 29
East Mount Rd *ACOMB* YO24 2
East Pde *HEWTH* YO31 3
Eastward Av *FUL/HES* YO10 24
East Wy *HEWTH* YO31 10
Eaton Ct *ACOMB* YO24 22
Ebor Pth *CYK* YO1 2
Ebor St *COP/BISH* YO23 2
Ebor Wy *COP/BISH* YO23 26
HXB/STR YO32 5
HXB/STR YO32 7
RYKW YO26 8
Ebsay Dr *RAW/SKEL* YO30 9
Eccles Cl *RAW/SKEL* YO30 9
Eden Cl *ACOMB* YO24 22
Edgerton Cl *TAD* LS24 30
Edgerton Ct *TAD* LS24 30
Edgerton Dr *TAD* LS24 30
Edgerton Garth *TAD* LS24 30
Edgware Rd *FUL/HES* YO10 24
Egremont Cl *STMFBR* YO41 15
Eighth Av *HEWTH* YO31 19
Elder Gv *HXB/STR* YO32 6
Eldon St *HEWTH* YO31 3
Eldon Ter *HEWTH* YO31 18
Eldwick Cl *RAW/SKEL* YO30 9
Elgar Cl *HEWTH* YO31 10
Elliot Ct *FUL/HES* YO10 24

Ell - Hel 35

lwood Ct *FUL/HES* YO10 * 24 B2
ma Gv *RAW/SKEL* YO30 ....9 F4
m End *HXB/STR* YO32.....................6 D1
mfield Av *HEWTH* YO31..................19 E1
mfield Ter *HEWTH* YO31................19 E2
m Gv *HEWTH* YO31........................11 E4
mlands Gv *HEWTH* YO31................19 E1
mpark Vw *HEWTH* YO31 ....19 F1
mpark Wy *HEWTH* YO31 ....19 F1
ne Elms *HXB/STR* YO32.................13 E2
m Tree Av *RYKW* YO26.....................8 A4
mtree Gdns *RYKW* YO26 ....16 D5
ston Cl *RAW/SKEL* YO30 ....17 H1
vington Ter *FUL/HES* YO10..............3 J5
wick Gv *FUL/HES* YO10 ....19 H5
nbleton Dr *RAW/SKEL* YO30.............9 G5
nerald St *HEWTH* YO31 ....18 C3
mily Ms *FUL/HES* YO10......................3 K6
nmerson St *HEWTH* YO31.................3 K2
nclosure Gdns *FUL/HES* YO10.......25 F3
ndfields Rd *FUL/HES* YO10 ....24 C4
nfield Crs *ACOMB* YO24..................23 F1
nnerdale Av *HEWTH* YO31 ....19 G4
scrick St *FUL/HES* YO10 ....3 H7
skdale Av *FUL/HES* YO10 ....25 G1
sk Dr *RYKW* YO26 ....16 C1
splanade Ct *RAW/SKEL* YO30 * 2 C3
tive Pl *ACOMB* YO24 ....22 B5
ton Dr *HXB/STR* YO32.......................6 B1
tty Av *FUL/HES* YO10......................19 F5
tty Cl *STMFBR* YO41 ....15 G3
va Av *RAW/SKEL* YO30......................9 E4
velyn Crs *RAW/SKEL* YO30 ....18 A2

F

aber Cl *COP/BISH* YO23 ....26 D4
aber St *HEWTH* YO31 ....3 J3
airfax *STMFBR* YO41 ....15 F3
airfax Cft *COP/BISH* YO23...............26 D5
airfax St *CYK* YO1 ....2 D6
airfield Rd *TAD* LS24 ....30 C3
airfields Dr *RAW/SKEL* YO30............8 C1
airfield Wy *TAD* LS24 ....30 C3
airway *RAW/SKEL* YO30 ....17 H1
irway Dr *RYKW* YO26........................8 A5
e Fairways *TAD* LS24......................30 C5
lcon Cl *HXB/STR* YO32 ....7 E2
lconer St *ACOMB* YO24 ....23 F1
lkland St *CYK* YO1 ....2 E6
lsgrave Crs *RAW/SKEL* YO30.......18 B2
rfield *RYKW* YO26............................16 D3
rfield La *RYKS* YO19......................21 G1
rmers Wy *COP/BISH* YO23 ....26 D4
rmlands Rd *ACOMB* YO24..............22 D4
rmstead Ri *HXB/STR* YO32 ....6 D4
rndale Av *FUL/HES* YO10 ....20 A5
rndale Cl *HXB/STR* YO32 ....7 E1
rndale St *FUL/HES* YO10 ....24 B2
rrar St *FUL/HES* YO10......................3 K7
rriers Cha *HXB/STR* YO32................5 F5
rriers Cft *COP/BISH* YO23 ....26 D4
wcett St *FUL/HES* YO10 ....3 H7
wkes Dr *RYKW* YO26......................16 D5
asegate *CYK* YO1 ....3 F4
llbrook Av *RYKW* YO26...................16 C5
nwick's La *FUL/HES* YO10.............24 B5
nwick St *COP/BISH* YO23 ....24 A2
rguson Wy *HXB/STR* YO32 ....11 E5
rn Cl *HXB/STR* YO32.......................11 F2
rn St *HEWTH* YO31 ....3 G1
rnway *FUL/HES* YO10......................25 G1
rry La *COP/BISH* YO23...................28 B3
rrymans Wk *RYKW* YO26 ....8 A3
tter La *CYK* YO1 ....2 E5
versham Crs *HEWTH* YO31 ....18 B2
wster Wy *FUL/HES* YO10.................3 G7
wston Dr *RAW/SKEL* YO30...............9 G5
eld Ct *HEWTH* YO31 * 19 F3
eld Dr *TAD* LS24 ....31 F1
eld La *FUL/HES* YO10......................25 G2
eld Vw *RAW/SKEL* YO30 ....18 B2
th Av *HEWTH* YO31 ....3 K2
ey Ter *RAW/SKEL* YO30..................18 B2
nsbury Av *COP/BISH* YO23 ....24 A3
nsbury St *COP/BISH* YO23 ....24 A3
rbank Cl *HXB/STR* YO32 ....5 F3
r Heath Cl *ACOMB* YO24 ....22 C3
rs Garth La *STMFBR* YO41 ....15 F2
rst Av *HEWTH* YO31 ....19 E3
tree Cl *ACOMB* YO24......................23 E1
HXB/STR YO32...................................7 F4
tree Crs *TAD* LS24 ....30 B4
wood Whin *HEWTH* YO31 ....11 E3
hergate *FUL/HES* YO10 ....3 G7
zroy Ter *FUL/HES* YO10 ....3 J7
vian Gv *RAW/SKEL* YO30................17 G1
Flaxman Av *FUL/HES* YO10..............19 F5
Flaxman Cft *COP/BISH* YO23..........26 D4
Flaxton Rd *HXB/STR* YO32...............5 H3
Fleming Av *HEWTH* YO31..................3 K2
Fletcher Ct *HXB/STR* YO32 ....6 C2
Fletcher's Cft *COP/BISH* YO23........27 E4
Florence Gv *RAW/SKEL* YO30 ....9 E4
Fold Wk *HXB/STR* YO32.....................5 H1
Folks Cl *HXB/STR* YO32.....................7 E2
Folly Br *RAW/SKEL* YO30...................8 B2
Fordlands Crs *RYKS* YO19..............29 E1
Fordlands Rd *RYKS* YO19................29 E1
Forest Cl *HXB/STR* YO32 ....6 B3
Forester's Wk *ACOMB* YO24............22 B3
STMFBR YO41....................................15 E4
Forestgate *HXB/STR* YO32 ....6 C4
Forest Gv *HEWTH* YO31....................19 E3
Forest La *RYKS* YO19.......................29 H3
Forest Wy *HEWTH* YO31..................19 E3
Forge Cl *HXB/STR* YO32 ....11 E4
Forth St *RYKW* YO26........................17 G3
Foss Bank *HEWTH* YO31....................3 H3
Foss Br *HXB/STR* YO32 ....5 E3
Foss Ct *HEWTH* YO31 ....10 D5
Fossgate *CYK* YO1 ....3 G4
Foss Islands Rd *HEWTH* YO31 ....3 J5
Fossland Vw *HXB/STR* YO32 ....5 F3
Foss Wk *RYKW* YO26........................16 C1
Foss Wy *FUL/HES* YO10.....................3 G7
Fossway *HEWTH* YO31.....................18 D2
STMFBR YO41....................................15 F4
Foston Gv *HEWTH* YO31..................19 E1
Fountayne St *HEWTH* YO31.............18 C2
Fourth Av *HEWTH* YO31 ....3 K3
Fox Covert *HEWTH* YO31 ....11 E4
Foxcroft *HXB/STR* YO32....................6 C5
Fox Garth *RYKW* YO26.......................8 B3
Fox Gld *STMFBR* YO41 ....15 E3
Foxthorn Paddock
FUL/HES YO10.................................25 H1
Foxton Cl *ACOMB* YO24...................22 C4
Foxwood La *ACOMB* YO24...............22 A3
Frances St *FUL/HES* YO10...............24 B3
Frazer Ct *RAW/SKEL* YO30 ....17 F1
Frederic St *RAW/SKEL* YO30 ....2 C3
Friargate *CYK* YO1 ....3 F5
Friar's Wk *HEWTH* YO31 ....18 D1
Front St *ACOMB* YO24 ....22 C1
Fryors Cl *RYKS* YO19 ....20 D4
Fulford Cross *FUL/HES* YO10..........24 B3
Fulfordgate *FUL/HES* YO10 ....24 C5
Fulford Pk *FUL/HES* YO10...............24 B5
Fulford Rd *FUL/HES* YO10 ....24 B4
Furlong Rd *STMFBR* YO41 ....15 G3
Furness Dr *RAW/SKEL* YO30 ....9 F5
Furnwood *HXB/STR* YO32 ....6 D4
Fylingdale Av *RAW/SKEL* YO30 ......17 F1

G

Gainsborough Cl *HXB/STR* YO32 .....5 H1
Gale Farm Ct *ACOMB* YO24.............22 C1
Gale La *ACOMB* YO24 ....22 C2
Galligap La *FUL/HES* YO10 ....19 H5
The Gallops *ACOMB* YO24 ....22 B4
Galmanhoe La *RAW/SKEL* YO30 ......2 D2
Galtres Av *HEWTH* YO31..................19 G2
Galtres Gv *RAW/SKEL* YO30............17 G2
Galtres Rd *HEWTH* YO31 ....19 G2
Ganton Pl *ACOMB* YO24 ....23 E5
Garbett Wy *COP/BISH* YO23 ....28 B4
Garburn Gv *RAW/SKEL* YO30 ....9 F5
Garbutt Gv *RYKW* YO26...................17 E4
Garden Ct *RYKW* YO26....................16 D4
Gardeners Cl *COP/BISH* YO23 ....26 D4
Garden Flats La *RYKS* YO19............21 H3
Garden Pl *CYK* YO1 ....3 G4
Garden St *HEWTH* YO31 ....3 F1
The Garden Village
HXB/STR YO32...................................7 G3
Garden Wy *RYKW* YO26...................16 D4
Garfield Ter *RYKW* YO26..................17 G4
The Garlands *RAW/SKEL* YO30 ....17 H1
Garland St *RYKW* YO26....................17 F5
Garnet Ter *RYKW* YO26....................17 F4
Garroway Wy *FUL/HES* YO10 ....25 F4
Garrowby Vw *STMFBR* YO41...........15 G2
Garrow Hl *FUL/HES* YO10................24 D2
Garrow Hill Av *FUL/HES* YO10 ....25 E1
Garth Rd *HXB/STR* YO32 ....11 F2
Garth's End *FUL/HES* YO10 ....24 C4
HXB/STR YO32...................................7 F2
Garth Ter *RAW/SKEL* YO30 ....18 A2
Garthway *HXB/STR* YO32................10 C3
Gascoigne Wk *COP/BISH* YO23 ....2 E7
Gateland Cl *HXB/STR* YO32 ....6 C4
Gay Mdw *HXB/STR* YO32.................13 E2
Geldof Rd *HXB/STR* YO32...............11 E5
George Caley Dr *RAW/SKEL* YO30...9 H3
George Cayley Dr
RAW/SKEL YO30 ....9 H3
George Ct *HEWTH* YO31 ....3 H2
George Hudson St *CYK* YO1 ....2 D5
George St *CYK* YO1 ....3 H6
Gerard Av *HEWTH* YO31 ....19 F3
Germany La *FUL/HES* YO10 ....29 E1
Giles Av *HEWTH* YO31 ....19 F4
Gillamoor Av *HEWTH* YO31 ....19 G4
Gillingwood Rd *RAW/SKEL* YO30 ....9 G4
Gillygate *HEWTH* YO31 ....2 E2
Girvan Cl *ACOMB* YO24 ....22 B5
Givendale Gv *FUL/HES* YO10 ....19 H5
The Glade *HEWTH* YO31 ....19 G2
Gladstone St *ACOMB* YO24 ....22 D1
HEWTH YO31 ....18 D3
Glaisby Ct *HEWTH* YO31 ....19 F3
Glaisdale Rd *RYKW* YO26................16 A3
Glebe Av *RYKW* YO26......................17 E4
Glebe Cl *HXB/STR* YO32 ....5 G3
Glebe Wy *HXB/STR* YO32..................6 C2
Glen Av *HEWTH* YO31.........................3 J2
Glen Cl *FUL/HES* YO10....................29 E1
Glencoe St *RAW/SKEL* YO30...........18 A2
Glenridding *ACOMB* YO24..............22 D5
Glen Rd *HEWTH* YO31 ....3 K2
Godwinsway *STMFBR* YO41 ....15 G3
Golf Links Av *TAD* LS24...................30 B4
Golf Links Ct *TAD* LS24...................30 C4
Golf Links Crs *TAD* LS24..................30 B4
Goodramgate *CYK* YO1 ....3 F4
Goodricke Wy *FUL/HES* YO10.........25 E3
Goodwood Gv *ACOMB* YO24 ....23 F3
Gordon St *FUL/HES* YO10..................3 J7
Gormire Av *HEWTH* YO31................10 D4
Gorse Hl *RYKS* YO19 ....21 H3
Gorse Paddock *HEWTH* YO31.........11 E4
Gouthwaith Cl *RAW/SKEL* YO30......9 G4
Government House Rd
RAW/SKEL YO30 * 2 A1
Gower Rd *ACOMB* YO24 ....23 E4
Grampian Cl *HXB/STR* YO32 ....11 E1
Granary Ct *CYK* YO1 ....3 G3
Grange Av *TAD* LS24........................31 E2
Grange Cl *RAW/SKEL* YO30..............8 C1
Grange Crs *TAD* LS24 ....30 D2
Grange Garth *FUL/HES* YO10..........24 B2
Grange La *COP/BISH* YO23.............22 A2
Granger Av *RYKW* YO26 ....16 D5
Grange Rd *TAD* LS24........................31 E2
Grange St *FUL/HES* YO10 * 24 C2
Grantham Dr *RYKW* YO26...............17 F5
Grants Av *FUL/HES* YO10 ....24 C4
Granville Ter *FUL/HES* YO10 ....3 K6
Grape La *CYK* YO1 ....3 F4
Grasmere Dr *FUL/HES* YO10 ....19 G5
Grasmere Gv *RAW/SKEL* YO30.........9 G5
Grassholme *ACOMB* YO24..............22 C5
Grayshon Dr *RYKW* YO26................16 C4
Gray St *COP/BISH* YO23 ....2 D7
Great North Wy *RYKW* YO26 ....16 D1
Greenacres *HXB/STR* YO32 ....11 E2
Greencliffe Dr *RAW/SKEL* YO30......17 H3
Green Cl *RAW/SKEL* YO30...............17 H1
Greencroft Ct *RYKS* YO19 ....21 H4
Greencroft La *RYKS* YO19 ....21 H4
Green Dike *HXB/STR* YO32................6 B3
Green Dykes La *FUL/HES* YO10 .....24 D1
Greenfield Park Dr
HEWTH YO31 ....19 F1
Greenfields *HEWTH* YO31 ....18 C2
Green La *ACOMB* YO24 ....22 D2
COP/BISH YO23...............................27 H2
HXB/STR YO32...................................6 A1
RAW/SKEL YO30................................9 G5
Green Mdw *HEWTH* YO31 ....19 F2
Greensborough Av *RYKW* YO26....16 C4
Greenshaw Dr *HXB/STR* YO32.........6 C2
Greenside *RYKS* YO19 ....21 H4
Greenside Cl *RYKS* YO19.................21 H4
Greenside Wk *RYKS* YO19 ....21 H4
Green Sward *HEWTH* YO31.............19 F2
The Green *RYKS* YO19 ....21 H4
RYKW YO26......................................22 C1
Green Wy *HXB/STR* YO32 ....11 E2
The Greenway *HXB/STR* YO32 ....6 C4
Greenwood Gv *ACOMB* YO24 ....22 C4
Gregory Cl *RAW/SKEL* YO30.............8 D1
Grenwich Cl *RAW/SKEL* YO30 ....9 F3
Gresley Ct *RYKW* YO26 ....16 C5
Greystoke Rd *RAW/SKEL* YO30........9 G5
Greystone Ct *HXB/STR* YO32...........6 C5
Grimwith Garth
RAW/SKEL YO30 * 9 G4
Grosvenor Rd *RAW/SKEL* YO30 .....18 B3
Grosvenor Ter *RAW/SKEL* YO30 ......2 D1
Grove Gdns *RYKW* YO26...................8 A5
Groves Ct *HEWTH* YO31 ....3 G2
Groves La *HEWTH* YO31 ....3 H1
Grove Terrace La *HEWTH* YO31.....18 C3
The Grove *ACOMB* YO24.................27 G1
Grove Vw *RAW/SKEL* YO30 ....17 H3

H

Hackness Rd *RYKW* YO26.................16 A3
Hadrian Av *FUL/HES* YO10 ....25 F1
Haley's Ter *HEWTH* YO31.................18 C1
Halifax Ct *RAW/SKEL* YO30 ....9 H5
Halladale Cl *ACOMB* YO24...............22 B5
Hallard Wy *HXB/STR* YO32................5 G3
Hallcroft La *COP/BISH* YO23...........26 C4
Hallfield Rd *HEWTH* YO31 ....3 K3
Hall Pk *FUL/HES* YO10 ....25 F3
Hall Ri *HXB/STR* YO32 ....6 D2
Hambleton Av *FUL/HES* YO10.........19 H5
Hambleton Ter *HEWTH* YO31 ....18 B2
Hambleton Vw *HXB/STR* YO32 ....6 B1
Hambleton Wy *HXB/STR* YO32 ......11 E3
Hamilton Dr *ACOMB* YO24 ....23 E2
Hamilton Dr East *ACOMB* YO24......23 F2
Hamilton Dr West *ACOMB* YO24...22 D2
Hamilton Wy *ACOMB* YO24.............23 E2
Hammerton Cl *RYKW* YO26 ....22 B1
Hampden St *CYK* YO1.......................2 E6
Handley Cl *RAW/SKEL* YO30.............9 H4
Hanover St East *RYKW* YO26..........17 G4
Hanover St West *RYKW* YO26 ....17 G4
Hansom Pl *HEWTH* YO31.................18 B2
Harcourt Cl *COP/BISH* YO23 ....28 A4
Harcourt St *HEWTH* YO31 ....3 K2
Harden Cl *RAW/SKEL* YO30 ....9 G4
Hardisty Ms *RYKW* YO26 ....17 G4
Hardrada Wy *STMFBR* YO41...........15 F4
Harewood Cl *HXB/STR* YO32 ....6 B1
RAW/SKEL YO30.................................9 E4
Harewood Wy *FUL/HES* YO10..........25 E2
Harington Av *FUL/HES* YO10...........19 E5
Harlow Cl *ACOMB* YO24..................23 F2
Harlow Ct *HXB/STR* YO32 ....5 F4
Harlow Rd *ACOMB* YO24 ....23 F2
Harold Ct *ACOMB* YO24 ....22 D1
Harolds Wy *STMFBR* YO41 ....15 F4
Harrison St *HEWTH* YO31 ....19 E3
Harrow Gld *RAW/SKEL* YO30 ....9 H5
Hartoft St *FUL/HES* YO10................24 B2
Harvest Cl *HXB/STR* YO32 ....5 G3
Harwood Rd *RYKW* YO26................16 A3
Hassacarr La *RYKS* YO19 ....21 H5
Hastings Cl *RAW/SKEL* YO30 ....9 H5
Hatfield Cl *RAW/SKEL* YO30 ....9 F3
Hatters Cl *COP/BISH* YO23 ....26 D4
Haughton Rd *RAW/SKEL* YO30......18 B2
Hawkshead Cl *ACOMB* YO24..........22 B4
Hawthorn Av *HXB/STR* YO32 ....6 D2
TAD LS24 ....30 B5
Hawthorn Cl *TAD* LS24 ....30 C5
Hawthorn Cft *TAD* LS24 ....30 B5
Hawthorne Cl *RYKW* YO26................8 A4
Hawthorne Ms *HXB/STR* YO32.........5 G3
Hawthorn Gv *HEWTH* YO31 ....3 J2
Hawthorn Spinney
HEWTH YO31 ....10 D3
Hawthorn St *HEWTH* YO31...............3 J2
Hawthorn Ter Central
HXB/STR YO32.................................10 C3
Hawthorn Ter North
HXB/STR YO32.................................10 D2
Hawthorn Ter South
HXB/STR YO32.................................10 C3
Haxby Moor Rd *HXB/STR* YO32 ......4 D3
Haxby Rd *HEWTH* YO31..................18 B3
Hazel Cl *HXB/STR* YO32 ....10 C4
Hazel Ct *FUL/HES* YO10....................3 K4
Hazel Garth *HEWTH* YO31..............19 G3
Hazelmere Ct *HXB/STR* YO32 ....10 D3
Hazelnut Gv *RAW/SKEL* YO30........10 A4
Hazelwood Av *FUL/HES* YO10........20 A5
Headland Cl *HXB/STR* YO32.............6 C2
Headley Cl *RAW/SKEL* YO30.............9 H5
Healey Gv *HEWTH* YO31 ....19 E1
Heath Cl *ACOMB* YO24...................23 F2
Heath Cft *FUL/HES* YO10................24 D5
Heather Bank *FUL/HES* YO10.........19 H5
STMFBR YO41..................................15 F3
Heather Cl *HXB/STR* YO32 ....11 F2
Heather Cft *HEWTH* YO31..............10 D4
Heatherdene *TAD* LS24 ....30 D2
Heathfield Rd *FUL/HES* YO10.........25 E1
Heath Moor Dr *FUL/HES* YO10......24 D4
Heath Ride *HXB/STR* YO32 ....5 H1
Hebdon Ri *ACOMB* YO24 ....22 D1
Helmsdale *ACOMB* YO24 ....26 D1
Helmsley Gv *HXB/STR* YO32 ....6 A2

36 Hem - Lov

Hemlock Av *HEWTH* YO31 10 D5
Hempland Av *HEWTH* YO31 19 E3
Hempland Dr *HEWTH* YO31 19 F2
Hempland La *HEWTH* YO31 19 F3
Hendon Garth *RAW/SKEL* YO30 9 H5
Herbert St *FUL/HES* YO10 3 K6
Herberts Wy *HEWTH* YO31 19 E2
Herdsman Dr *COP/BISH* YO23 27 E4
Herdsman Rd *ACOMB* YO24 22 D4
Herdwick Cl *RAW/SKEL* YO30 10 A5
Herman Wk *ACOMB* YO24 22 C4
Heron Av *ACOMB* YO24 22 C4
Heron Ri *HXB/STR* YO32 11 E1
Hesketh Bank *FUL/HES* YO10 25 H1
Heslin Cl *HXB/STR* YO32 6 C3
Heslington Ct *FUL/HES* YO10 25 F3
Heslington Cft *FUL/HES* YO10 24 D5
Heslington La *FUL/HES* YO10 24 C5
Heslington Rd *FUL/HES* YO10 3 J7
Hessay Pl *RYKW* YO26 22 A1
Hetherton St *RAW/SKEL* YO30 2 C3
Hewley Av *FUL/HES* YO10 19 E5
Heworth *HEWTH* YO31 19 E3
Heworth Gn *HEWTH* YO31 3 J1
Heworth Hall Dr *HEWTH* YO31 19 F3
Heworth Ms *HEWTH* YO31 3 J2
Heworth Pl *HEWTH* YO31 19 E3
Heworth Rd *HEWTH* YO31 19 E3
Heworth Village *HEWTH* YO31 * 19 E3
High Catton Rd *STMFBR* YO41 15 F4
Highcliffe Ct *RAW/SKEL* YO30 17 H3
High Fld *FUL/HES* YO10 20 A5
Highgrove Cl *RAW/SKEL* YO30 9 F3
Highlands Av *HXB/STR* YO32 5 G3
Highmoor Cl *ACOMB* YO24 22 D4
Highmoor Rd *ACOMB* YO24 22 D4
High Newbiggin St *HEWTH* YO31 3 G2
High Oaks *HEWTH* YO31 19 G2
High Ousegate *CYK* YO1 3 F5
High Petergate *CYK* YO1 2 E3
High St *TAD* LS24 30 C3
Highthorn Rd *HEWTH* YO31 10 D4
Hilbeck Gv *HEWTH* YO31 19 G3
Hilbra Av *HXB/STR* YO32 6 D5
Hilda St *FUL/HES* YO10 3 K6
Hillary Garth *RYKW* YO26 17 F5
Hill Crest *RYKS* YO19 13 H5
Hillcrest *TAD* LS24 30 B4
Hillcrest Av *RYKW* YO26 8 B4
Hillcrest Ct *TAD* LS24 30 B4
Hill Crest Gdns *ACOMB* YO24 23 F3
Hillsborough Ter
RAW/SKEL YO30 18 B2
Hill St *ACOMB* YO24 23 E1
Hill Vw *HEWTH* YO31 19 H2
Hinton Av *ACOMB* YO24 22 C4
Hobgate *ACOMB* YO24 22 D1
Hob Moor Dr *ACOMB* YO24 23 E2
Hobmoor Ter *ACOMB* YO24 23 F3
Holburns Cft *FUL/HES* YO10 25 F3
Holgate Bridge Gdn
ACOMB YO24 2 A7
Holgate Lodge Dr *RYKW* YO26 17 F5
Holgate Park Dr *RYKW* YO26 17 G5
Holgate Rd *ACOMB* YO24 23 F1
Hollis Crs *HXB/STR* YO32 5 G4
Holly Bank Gv *ACOMB* YO24 23 F2
Holly Bank Rd *ACOMB* YO24 23 F2
Hollyrood Dr *RAW/SKEL* YO30 9 F3
Holly Ter *FUL/HES* YO10 * 24 A3
Holly Tree Cft *RYKS* YO19 21 H3
Holly Tree Garth *HXB/STR* YO32 13 E1
Holly Tree La *HXB/STR* YO32 6 D3
RYKS YO19 21 H3
Holmefield La *FUL/HES* YO10 25 E3
Holroyd Av *HEWTH* YO31 19 F4
Holtby La *HXB/STR* YO32 12 C4
RYKS YO19 13 E5
Homefield Cl *COP/BISH* YO23 26 C5
Homelea *HXB/STR* YO32 5 F4
Homestead Cl *HXB/STR* YO32 11 E5
Hope St *FUL/HES* YO10 3 H6
Hopgrove La *HXB/STR* YO32 12 B4
Hopgrove La North
HXB/STR YO32 11 H3
Hopgrove La South
HXB/STR YO32 12 A3
Hornbeam Cl *RAW/SKEL* YO30 10 A4
Horner St *RAW/SKEL* YO30 18 A2
Hornsey Garth *HXB/STR* YO32 6 C2
Horseman Av *COP/BISH* YO23 26 C4
Horseman Cl *COP/BISH* YO23 26 C4
Horseman Dr *COP/BISH* YO23 26 C4
Horseman La *COP/BISH* YO23 26 C4
The Horseshoe *ACOMB* YO24 23 E5
Horsfield Wy *RYKS* YO19 21 H3
Horsman Av *FUL/HES* YO10 3 H7
Hospital Fields Rd
FUL/HES YO10 24 B3
Hotham Av *RYKW* YO26 22 B2
Hothams Ct *CYK* YO1 * 3 G5
Houndsway *ACOMB* YO24 22 B4
Howard Dr *RAW/SKEL* YO30 9 E4
Howard Link *RAW/SKEL* YO30 9 F4
Howard Rd *HXB/STR* YO32 5 H4
Howard St *FUL/HES* YO10 24 B2
Howe Hill Cl *RYKW* YO26 17 F5
Howe Hill Rd *RYKW* YO26 17 F5
Howe St *ACOMB* YO24 22 D1
Hubert St *COP/BISH* YO23 23 H3
Huby Ct *CYK* YO1 3 J6
Hudson Cl *STMFBR* YO41 15 G3
TAD LS24 30 D1
Hudson Crs *RAW/SKEL* YO30 17 H2
Hudson St *RAW/SKEL* YO30 18 B2
Hudson Vw *TAD* LS24 30 D2
Hudson Wy *RYKW* YO26 16 D1
TAD LS24 30 D1
Hull Rd *FUL/HES* YO10 25 G1
RYKS YO19 21 F5
Humber Dr *HXB/STR* YO32 5 G4
Hungate *CYK* YO1 3 G4
Hunt Ct *CYK* YO1 * 3 G3
Hunters Cl *HXB/STR* YO32 6 C3
RYKS YO19 21 F4
Hunters Wy *ACOMB* YO24 23 F5
Hunters Wood Wy *RYKS* YO19 21 G4
Huntington Ms *HEWTH* YO31 * 18 C2
Huntington Rd *HEWTH* YO31 3 H1
HXB/STR YO32 10 D3
Huntsmans La *STMFBR* YO41 15 E3
Huntsman's Wk *ACOMB* YO24 22 C3
Hurricane Wy *RAW/SKEL* YO30 9 F3
Hurst's Yd *CYK* YO1 3 H5
Hutton Cl *RYKW* YO26 8 B4
Hyrst Gv *HEWTH* YO31 18 D3

I

Ikin Wy *HXB/STR* YO32 7 F5
Ilton Garth *RAW/SKEL* YO30 9 H4
Ingleborough Av
FUL/HES YO10 19 G5
Ingleby Dr *TAD* LS24 30 D2
Ingleton Wk *HEWTH* YO31 19 F4
Ingram Av *RAW/SKEL* YO30 18 B1
Ings La *RYKW* YO26 8 C5
Ings Vw *RAW/SKEL* YO30 9 E4
Ings Wy *RAW/SKEL* YO30 17 G1
Inholmes La *TAD* LS24 30 B3
Inman Ter *RYKW* YO26 17 E5
Innovation Cl *FUL/HES* YO10 25 F2
Innovation Wy *FUL/HES* YO10 25 F2
Intake Av *RAW/SKEL* YO30 18 B1
Intake La *RYKS* YO19 21 H4
Invicta Ct *ACOMB* YO24 22 B4
Irwin Av *HEWTH* YO31 18 D3
Iver Cl *RYKW* YO26 16 D4

J

Jackson St *HEWTH* YO31 3 G1
Jacobi Cl *RAW/SKEL* YO30 17 H2
James Backhouse Pl
ACOMB YO24 23 E1
James Nicholson Link
RAW/SKEL YO30 9 H4
James St *FUL/HES* YO10 3 J4
James Wy *FUL/HES* YO10 25 E3
Jamieson Ter *COP/BISH* YO23 23 H3
Jasmine Cl *HXB/STR* YO32 10 C4
Jaywick Cl *HXB/STR* YO32 5 G1
Jedwell Cl *HXB/STR* YO32 10 C1
Jennifer Gv *ACOMB* YO24 23 F2
Jervis Rd *ACOMB* YO24 23 E4
Jewbury *CYK* YO1 3 G3
Jockey La *HXB/STR* YO32 11 G5
John Saville Ct *CYK* YO1 * 3 G3
John St *HEWTH* YO31 3 K1
John Ward Cl *STMFBR* YO41 15 G3
Jorvic Cl *RYKW* YO26 16 D4
Julia Av *HXB/STR* YO32 11 G4
Juniper Cl *HXB/STR* YO32 10 C3
Jute Rd *RYKW* YO26 16 C5

K

Kathryn Av *HXB/STR* YO32 11 F4
Keats Cl *RAW/SKEL* YO30 9 G5
Keble Cl *COP/BISH* YO23 28 B4
Keble Dr *COP/BISH* YO23 28 A4
Keble Gdns *COP/BISH* YO23 28 B5
Keble Park Crs *COP/BISH* YO23 28 A5
Keble Pk North *COP/BISH* YO23 28 B4
Keble Pk South *COP/BISH* YO23 28 B5
Keith Av *HXB/STR* YO32 11 F2
Kelcbar Cl *TAD* LS24 30 B2
Kelcbar Hl *TAD* LS24 30 A2
Kelcbar Wy *TAD* LS24 30 B2
Keldale *HXB/STR* YO32 7 E1
Kempton Cl *ACOMB* YO24 22 D3
Kendal Cl *RYKS* YO19 21 H3
Kendrew Cl *HXB/STR* YO32 11 E3
Kenlay Cl *HXB/STR* YO32 10 C2
Kennedy Dr *HXB/STR* YO32 6 D2
Kenrick Pl *RYKW* YO26 16 D4
Kensal Ri *FUL/HES* YO10 24 B2
Kensington Ct *ACOMB* YO24 23 F4
Kensington Rd *RAW/SKEL* YO30 9 E4
Kensington St *COP/BISH* YO23 23 H3
Kentmere Dr *RAW/SKEL* YO30 9 G5
Kent St *FUL/HES* YO10 3 H7
Kerrside *RAW/SKEL* YO30 17 F1
Kerver La *RYKS* YO19 21 H3
Kestrel Wood Wy *HEWTH* YO31 11 E4
Keswick Wy *HXB/STR* YO32 11 E1
Kettleman Br *TAD* LS24 31 E5
Kettlestring La *RAW/SKEL* YO30 9 H3
Kexby Av *FUL/HES* YO10 24 D1
Key Wy *RYKS* YO19 29 F2
Kilburn Rd *FUL/HES* YO10 24 B2
Kimberlows Wood Hl
FUL/HES YO10 25 G1
Kinbrace Dr *ACOMB* YO24 22 B5
Kings Acre *HEWTH* YO31 19 G3
Kingsclere *HXB/STR* YO32 7 F5
Kings Ct *CYK* YO1 3 F4
Kingsland Ter *RYKW* YO26 17 G4
Kings Moor Rd *HXB/STR* YO32 12 D2
King's Sq *CYK* YO1 3 F4
Kings Staith *CYK* YO1 3 F5
Kingsthorpe *ACOMB* YO24 22 D2
King St *CYK* YO1 3 F5
Kingsway *STMFBR* YO41 15 G2
Kingsway North
RAW/SKEL YO30 18 A2
Kingsway West *ACOMB* YO24 22 D3
Kingswood Gv *ACOMB* YO24 22 D2
Kir Crs *ACOMB* YO24 22 C1
Kirkcroft *HXB/STR* YO32 6 C3
Kirkdale Rd *FUL/HES* YO10 20 A5
Kirkgate *TAD* LS24 30 D3
Kirkham Av *HEWTH* YO31 18 D1
Kirklands *HXB/STR* YO32 5 G4
Kirkstone Dr *HEWTH* YO31 19 F3
Kirk Vw *RYKW* YO26 22 C1
Kirkwell *COP/BISH* YO23 28 A3
Kitchener St *HEWTH* YO31 18 C2
Kitemere Pl *ACOMB* YO24 22 B4
Knapton Cl *HXB/STR* YO32 5 G4
Knapton La *RYKW* YO26 16 C5
Knavesmire Crs *COP/BISH* YO23 23 H3
Knavesmire Rd *ACOMB* YO24 23 G2
The Knoll *ACOMB* YO24 22 B3
Kyle Wy *RYKW* YO26 16 C1
Kyme St *CYK* YO1 2 E6

L

Laburnum Garth *HEWTH* YO31 19 E1
Lady Hamilton Gdns
ACOMB YO24 22 D2
Lady Rd *RAW/SKEL* YO30 18 A2
Ladysmith Ms *HXB/STR* YO32 5 F3
Lakeside Ct *ACOMB* YO24 * 23 F4
Lakeside Gdns *HXB/STR* YO32 5 H1
Lambert Ct *CYK* YO1 2 E6
Lamel St *FUL/HES* YO10 25 E1
Lamplugh Crs *COP/BISH* YO23 28 B4
Lancar Cl *HXB/STR* YO32 6 A2
Lancaster Vls *RYKW* YO26 * 8 A5
Lancaster Wy *RAW/SKEL* YO30 9 H5
Landalewood Rd
RAW/SKEL YO30 9 G4
Landau Cl *RAW/SKEL* YO30 17 G1
Landing La *HXB/STR* YO32 7 E4
RYKW YO26 17 F4
The Landings *HXB/STR* YO32 7 E2
The Lane *STMFBR* YO41 14 A3
Lang Av *FUL/HES* YO10 19 F5
Langdale Av *HEWTH* YO31 19 G3
Langholme Dr *RYKW* YO26 16 D3
Langley Ct *HXB/STR* YO32 11 E1
Lang Rd *COP/BISH* YO23 27 H3
HXB/STR YO32 7 F5
Langsett Gv *RAW/SKEL* YO30 9 G3
Langton Ct *HXB/STR* YO32 5 F4
Lansdowne Ter *FUL/HES* YO10 3 K6
Lansdown Wy *HXB/STR* YO32 7 E2
Lanshaw Cft *RAW/SKEL* YO30 9
Larchfield *HEWTH* YO31 19
Larch Wy *HXB/STR* YO32 6
Larkfield Cl *COP/BISH* YO23 26
Lastingham Ter
FUL/HES YO10 * 24
Laurel Cl *HXB/STR* YO32 7
Lavender Gv *RYKW* YO26 17
Lawnswood Dr *RAW/SKEL* YO30 17
Lawnway *HEWTH* YO31 19
Lawrence Ct *FUL/HES* YO10 3
Lawrence St *FUL/HES* YO10 3
Lawson Rd *ACOMB* YO24 23
Layerthorpe *CYK* YO1 3
Lead Mill La *CYK* YO1 3
Leake St *FUL/HES* YO10 3
Learmans Wy *COP/BISH* YO23 27
Lea Wy *HXB/STR* YO32 11
Leeds Rd *TAD* LS24 30
Leeman Rd *RYKW* YO26 2
Leeside *ACOMB* YO24 23
Leicester Wy *CYK* YO1 * 3
Leighton Cft *RAW/SKEL* YO30 9
Lendal *CYK* YO1 2
Lendal Br *CYK* YO1 2
Lerecroft Rd *ACOMB* YO24 22
Lesley Av *FUL/HES* YO10 24
Leven Rd *ACOMB* YO24 22
Levisham St *FUL/HES* YO10 24
The Leyes *FUL/HES* YO10 19
Leyfield Cl *HXB/STR* YO32 5
Leyland Rd *HEWTH* YO31 19
Lichfield Ct *COP/BISH* YO23 23
Lidgett Gv *RYKW* YO26 16
Lilac Av *FUL/HES* YO10 25
Lilac Gv *HXB/STR* YO32 10
Lilbourne Dr *RAW/SKEL* YO30 17
Lilling Av *HEWTH* YO31 18
Lime Av *HEWTH* YO31 19
Limegarth *RYKW* YO26 8
The Limes *HXB/STR* YO32 12
Lime Tree Av *HXB/STR* YO32 10
Lime Tree Ms *RYKS* YO19 21
Lincoln St *RYKW* YO26 17
Lindale *ACOMB* YO24 22
Linden Cl *HXB/STR* YO32 11
Linden Gv *RAW/SKEL* YO30 17
Lindley Rd *RAW/SKEL* YO30 9
Lindley St *ACOMB* YO24 23
Lindley Wood Gv
RAW/SKEL YO30 9
Lindsey Av *RYKW* YO26 17
Lingcroft La *RYKS* YO19 29
Lingfield Crs *ACOMB* YO24 23
Link Av *RAW/SKEL* YO30 18
Link Rd *HXB/STR* YO32 10
Link Road Ct *FUL/HES* YO10 20
The Links *TAD* LS24 30
The Link *COP/BISH* YO23 26
FUL/HES YO10 24
Linley Av *HXB/STR* YO32 7
Linnet Wy *ACOMB* YO24 22
Linton Rd *RYKW* YO26 8
Linton St *RYKW* YO26 17
Lister Ct *RYKW* YO26 * 17
Lister Wy *RAW/SKEL* YO30 17
Little Av *RAW/SKEL* YO30 18
Little Catterton La *TAD* LS24 31
Littlefield Cl *RYKW* YO26 8
Little Garth *RYKW* YO26 8
Little Hallfield Rd *HEWTH* YO31 3
Little La *HXB/STR* YO32 6
Little Mdw *HXB/STR* YO32 6
Little Shambles *CYK* YO1 3
Little Stonegate *CYK* YO1 2
Littlethorpe Cl *HXB/STR* YO32 5
Livingstone St *RYKW* YO26 17
Lloyd Cl *FUL/HES* YO10 25
Lob La *STMFBR* YO41 15
Lochrin Pl *RYKW* YO26 16
Lockey Cft *HXB/STR* YO32 6
Lock House La *HXB/STR* YO32 7
Lockwood St *HEWTH* YO31 3
Lockyer Cl *RAW/SKEL* YO30 17
Long Close La *FUL/HES* YO10 3
Longcroft *HXB/STR* YO32 6
Longfield Ter *RAW/SKEL* YO30 2
Long Furrow *HXB/STR* YO32 6
Long Ridge Dr *RYKW* YO26 8
Longridge Gdns *RYKW* YO26 8
Long Ridge La *RYKW* YO26 8
Longwood Link *RAW/SKEL* YO30 9
Longwood Rd *RAW/SKEL* YO30 9
Lord Mayor's Wk *HEWTH* YO31 3
Lords Moor La *HXB/STR* YO32 5
Loriners Dr *COP/BISH* YO23 26
Lorne St *COP/BISH* YO23 23
Love La *ACOMB* YO24 2
FUL/HES YO10 24

vell St *COP/BISH* YO23 24 A2
w Catton Rd *STMFBR* YO41 15 F4
w Cft *HXB/STR* YO32 5 F3
wer Darnborough St
COP/BISH YO23 3 F7
wer Ebor St *COP/BISH* YO23 24 A2
wer Friargate *CYK* YO1 3 F5
wer Priory St *CYK* YO1 2 D6
weswater Rd *RAW/SKEL* YO30 9 F5
wfield Dr *HXB/STR* YO32 6 D1
wfield La *RYKW* YO26 16 A5
wfields Dr *ACOMB* YO24 22 C2
w Gn *COP/BISH* YO23 26 D5
wick *ACOMB* YO24 22 C5
w La *FUL/HES* YO10 25 G3
w Mill Cl *FUL/HES* YO10 25 H1
w Moor Av *FUL/HES* YO10 24 D5
wn Hl *ACOMB* YO24 22 C2
w Ousegate *CYK* YO1 2 E5
w Petergate *CYK* YO1 3 F3
w Poppleton La *RYKW* YO26 16 C2
wther Ct *HEWTH* YO31 3 H1
wther Ms *HEWTH* YO31 * 18 B3
wther St *HEWTH* YO31 18 B3
wther Ter *ACOMB* YO24 2 B6
xley Cl *RAW/SKEL* YO30 9 G4
cas Av *RAW/SKEL* YO30 18 B1
combe Wy *HXB/STR* YO32 10 C2
mley Rd *RAW/SKEL* YO30 18 A2
nd Cl *HXB/STR* YO32 6 C3
nds Ct *CYK* YO1 * 3 F4
ndy Cl *RAW/SKEL* YO30 9 H5
cett Rd *ACOMB* YO24 23 F5
dham Ct *ACOMB* YO24 22 C4
ndale Av *FUL/HES* YO10 25 G1
nden Wy *ACOMB* YO24 22 D1
nwood Av *COP/BISH* YO23 26 C4
nwood Cl *HXB/STR* YO32 5 F3
nwood Vw *COP/BISH* YO23 26 C4
sander Cl *RAW/SKEL* YO30 9 H3

M

aclagan Rd *COP/BISH* YO23 27 H3
agnolia Gv *HXB/STR* YO32 10 C4
aida Gv *FUL/HES* YO10 24 B2
ain Av *HEWTH* YO31 19 E4
ain St *COP/BISH* YO23 26 B2
COP/BISH YO23 26 C5
COP/BISH YO23 28 A3
FUL/HES YO10 24 B5
FUL/HES YO10 25 F4
RYKW YO26 8 A4
RYKW YO26 16 A4
STMFBR YO41 15 G2
albys Gv *COP/BISH* YO23 26 D5
alham Gv *HEWTH* YO31 19 G4
allard Wy *HXB/STR* YO32 7 E2
allory Cl *HXB/STR* YO32 10 C2
alton Av *HEWTH* YO31 18 D3
alton Rd *HEWTH* YO31 19 E2
alton Wy *RAW/SKEL* YO30 17 G1
alvern Av *RYKW* YO26 17 E5
alvern Cl *HXB/STR* YO32 11 F1
ancroft *HXB/STR* YO32 6 C3
anley Cl *HXB/STR* YO32 10 C2
e Manor Beeches *RYKS* YO19 21 G3
anor Cl *RYKW* YO26 16 A1
anor Ct *FUL/HES* YO10 24 D1
HXB/STR YO32 11 E1
anor Dr *RYKS* YO19 21 G4
anor Dr North *RYKW* YO26 17 E5
anor Dr South *RYKW* YO26 17 E5
anor Farm Cl *COP/BISH* YO23 26 C5
anor Garth *HXB/STR* YO32 6 C3
nor Heath *COP/BISH* YO23 26 B4
nor La *RAW/SKEL* YO30 9 E4
nor Park Cl *RAW/SKEL* YO30 9 F4
nor Park Gv *RAW/SKEL* YO30 9 F4
nor Park Rd *RAW/SKEL* YO30 9 E4
nor Rd *TAD* LS24 30 D2
nor Wy *RAW/SKEL* YO30 9 F4
nsfield St *HEWTH* YO31 3 H3
nthorpe Wk *RYKW* YO26 17 F5
ple Av *COP/BISH* YO23 28 A4
ple Ct *FUL/HES* YO10 29 E1
ple Gv *FUL/HES* YO10 24 B3
plehurst Av *HEWTH* YO31 18 C2
plewood Paddock
ACOMB YO24 22 C3
rch St *HEWTH* YO31 3 G1
rgaret Philipson Ct *CYK* YO1 * 3 G3
rgaret St *FUL/HES* YO10 3 H6
rket St *CYK* YO1 3 F4
rkham Crs *HEWTH* YO31 18 C3
rkham St *HEWTH* YO31 18 B3
rlborough Av *TAD* LS24 30 B4

Marlborough Cl *RAW/SKEL* YO30 9 E3
Marlborough Dr *TAD* LS24 30 B4
Marlborough Gv *FUL/HES* YO10 24 B2
Marlborough Vls
FUL/HES YO10 * 24 B2
Marmiam Dr *HXB/STR* YO32 12 D2
Marston Av *RYKW* YO26 22 B1
Marston Crs *RYKW* YO26 22 B1
Martello Wy *HXB/STR* YO32 11 F5
Marten Cl *RAW/SKEL* YO30 17 H1
Martin Cheeseman Ct
ACOMB YO24 22 C4
Martins Ct *RYKW* YO26 17 H4
Marygate *RAW/SKEL* YO30 2 D3
Marygate La *RAW/SKEL* YO30 2 C2
Matmer Ct *FUL/HES* YO10 * 24 D1
Mattison Wy *ACOMB* YO24 23 E2
Mayfield Gv *ACOMB* YO24 23 F4
Maythorn Rd *HEWTH* YO31 10 D5
Meadlands *HEWTH* YO31 19 G3
Meadowbeck Cl *FUL/HES* YO10 19 G5
Meadow Ct *ACOMB* YO24 23 E4
Meadowfields Dr *HEWTH* YO31 10 C4
Meadow Garth *TAD* LS24 31 E2
Meadow La *HXB/STR* YO32 6 D3
The Meadows *RAW/SKEL* YO30 8 C1
Meadow Wy *HEWTH* YO31 19 E2
HXB/STR YO32 11 E2
TAD LS24 31 E2
Meam Cl *FUL/HES* YO10 20 B5
Melander Cl *RYKW* YO26 16 C5
Melander Gdns *HXB/STR* YO32 6 D4
Melbourne Ct *FUL/HES* YO10 * 24 B2
Melbourne St *FUL/HES* YO10 24 B2
Melcombe Av *HXB/STR* YO32 5 F3
Melrose Cl *HEWTH* YO31 19 E4
Melrosegate *FUL/HES* YO10 19 E5
Melroses Yd *CYK* YO1 * 3 H5
Melton Av *RAW/SKEL* YO30 17 G1
Melton Dr *COP/BISH* YO23 28 A4
RAW/SKEL YO30 17 G1
Melwood Gv *RYKW* YO26 16 C4
Mendip Cl *HXB/STR* YO32 11 E1
Merchantgate *CYK* YO1 3 G5
Merchant Wy *COP/BISH* YO23 26 D4
Merlin Covert *HEWTH* YO31 11 E3
Metcalfe La *RYKS* YO19 19 H4
The Mews *RAW/SKEL* YO30 * 17 H3
Micklegate *CYK* YO1 2 E5
Middle Banks *HXB/STR* YO32 6 B2
Middlecroft Dr *HXB/STR* YO32 5 F3
Middlecroft Gv *HXB/STR* YO32 5 F3
Middleham Av *HEWTH* YO31 18 D1
Middlethorpe Dr *ACOMB* YO24 23 F5
Middlethorpe Gv *ACOMB* YO24 23 F5
Middleton Rd *ACOMB* YO24 22 D2
Midgley Cl *STMFBR* YO41 15 G3
Midway Av *RYKW* YO26 8 B5
Mildred Gv *ACOMB* YO24 23 F2
Milford Wy *HXB/STR* YO32 6 D4
Millennium Ct *HEWTH* YO31 * 3 J3
Millers Cft *COP/BISH* YO23 26 D4
Millfield Av *FUL/HES* YO10 24 D1
Millfield Gdns *RYKW* YO26 8 B4
Millfield La *FUL/HES* YO10 25 E1
RYKW YO26 8 B4
Millfield Rd *COP/BISH* YO23 23 H2
Millgates *RYKW* YO26 16 D3
Mill Hill Dr *HXB/STR* YO32 11 E2
Mill La *COP/BISH* YO23 26 B3
HEWTH YO31 3 K1
HXB/STR YO32 6 A2
TAD LS24 30 D2
Mill Mt *ACOMB* YO24 2 B7
Mill Mount Ct *ACOMB* YO24 2 B7
Mill St *CYK* YO1 3 G6
Milner St *ACOMB* YO24 22 D1
Milson Gv *FUL/HES* YO10 25 E1
Milton Carr *RAW/SKEL* YO30 9 G5
Milton St *FUL/HES* YO10 24 D1
Minchin Cl *RAW/SKEL* YO30 10 A5
Minister Wy *CYK* YO1 3 G4
FUL/HES YO10 24 B5
Minster Av *HEWTH* YO31 11 E4
Minster Cl *HXB/STR* YO32 6 C3
Minster Ct *CYK* YO1 3 F2
Minster Gates *CYK* YO1 * 3 F3
Minster Vw *HXB/STR* YO32 6 C3
Minster Wy *CYK* YO1 3 F3
FUL/HES YO10 24 B2
STMFBR YO41 14 D4
Minster Yd *CYK* YO1 2 E3
Minter Cl *ACOMB* YO24 22 B3
Mistral Ct *HEWTH* YO31 18 D1
Mitchel's La *FUL/HES* YO10 24 D4
Miterdale *ACOMB* YO24 22 C5
Mitford Ms *HXB/STR* YO32 6 D4
Moat Fld *FUL/HES* YO10 19 H5
Moatside Ct *HEWTH* YO31 2 E2

Moins Ct *FUL/HES* YO10 25 H1
Moiser Cl *HXB/STR* YO32 10 C2
Monarch Wy *RYKW* YO26 17 E3
Monk Av *HEWTH* YO31 19 E2
Monk Bar Ct *CYK* YO1 3 G3
Monk Br *HEWTH* YO31 3 H2
Monkbridge Ct *HEWTH* YO31 3 H1
Monkgate *HEWTH* YO31 3 G2
Monkgate Cloisters
HEWTH YO31 3 G2
Monks Cross Dr *HXB/STR* YO32 11 G4
Monks Cross Link
HXB/STR YO32 11 G2
Monkton Rd *HEWTH* YO31 18 D1
Montague Rd *COP/BISH* YO23 28 A4
Montague St *COP/BISH* YO23 24 A3
Montague Wk *RYKW* YO26 8 A4
Montrose Av *HEWTH* YO31 18 C1
Moorcroft Rd *ACOMB* YO24 22 D5
Moore Av *FUL/HES* YO10 19 G5
Moorgarth Av *ACOMB* YO24 23 F2
Moorgate *ACOMB* YO24 22 D1
Moor Gv *ACOMB* YO24 23 E4
Moorland Garth *HXB/STR* YO32 5 F2
Moorland Rd *FUL/HES* YO10 24 B4
Moor La *ACOMB* YO24 26 C1
COP/BISH YO23 27 G5
HXB/STR YO32 4 A3
HXB/STR YO32 5 G3
HXB/STR YO32 7 G2
RYKS YO19 20 C1
RYKW YO26 16 A4
Moorlea Av *ACOMB* YO24 23 E4
Moor Rd *STMFBR* YO41 15 G3
Moor Wy *HXB/STR* YO32 11 F2
Morcar Rd *STMFBR* YO41 15 G3
Morehall Cl *RAW/SKEL* YO30 9 G4
Morrell Ct *ACOMB* YO24 22 B4
Morrell Wy *FUL/HES* YO10 25 E2
Morritt Cl *HEWTH* YO31 19 E1
Moss St *COP/BISH* YO23 2 C6
Mount Ephraim *ACOMB* YO24 2 B6
Mount Pde *ACOMB* YO24 2 B7
Mount Ter *ACOMB* YO24 * 2 B7
The Mount *ACOMB* YO24 2 B7
Mount V *ACOMB* YO24 23 G2
Mount Vale Dr *ACOMB* YO24 23 G2
Mowbray Dr *RYKW* YO26 16 D5
Muirfield Wy *RYKW* YO26 16 C4
Mulberry Ct *HXB/STR* YO32 7 F5
Mulberry Dr *HXB/STR* YO32 6 D1
Mulwith Cl *HEWTH* YO31 19 F3
Muncastergate *HEWTH* YO31 18 D2
Murray St *ACOMB* YO24 23 F1
Murrough Wilson Pl
HEWTH YO31 18 B2
Murton Garth *RYKS* YO19 20 C3
Murton La *RYKS* YO19 20 D4
Murton Wy *RYKS* YO19 20 A5
Museum St *CYK* YO1 2 E4
Myrtle Av *COP/BISH* YO23 28 B4

N

Naburn La *RYKS* YO19 28 D3
Nairn Cl *ACOMB* YO24 27 E1
Navigation Rd *CYK* YO1 3 H5
Nelson's La *ACOMB* YO24 23 F3
Nelson St *HEWTH* YO31 18 C3
Nessgate *CYK* YO1 3 F5
Nether Wy *RYKW* YO26 8 A4
Netherwindings *HXB/STR* YO32 7 F2
Netherwoods *HXB/STR* YO32 5 G1
Neville Dr *COP/BISH* YO23 28 A4
Neville St *HEWTH* YO31 18 C3
Neville Ter *HEWTH* YO31 18 C3
Nevinson Gv *FUL/HES* YO10 24 C4
Nevis Wy *ACOMB* YO24 22 B5
Newborough St
RAW/SKEL YO30 18 A3
Newbury Av *ACOMB* YO24 22 D3
Newby Ter *HEWTH* YO31 18 B2
Newdale *HXB/STR* YO32 7 E1
New Forge Ct *HXB/STR* YO32 7 F2
Newgate *CYK* YO1 * 3 F4
Newland Park Cl *FUL/HES* YO10 25 E1
Newland Park Dr
FUL/HES YO10 24 D2
Newlands Dr *RYKW* YO26 16 C3
Newlands Rd *COP/BISH* YO23 27 H3
New La *ACOMB* YO24 23 E1
COP/BISH YO23 27 H3
HXB/STR YO32 5 G1
HXB/STR YO32 11 E5
New St *CYK* YO1 2 E4
TAD LS24 30 D3
Newton Ter *CYK* YO1 2 E6

Newton Wy *HXB/STR* YO32 5 G4
New Walk Ter *FUL/HES* YO10 24 B2
Nicholas Gdns *FUL/HES* YO10 24 D1
Nicholas St *FUL/HES* YO10 24 D1
Nidd Cl *RYKW* YO26 16 C1
Nidd Gv *ACOMB* YO24 23 E5
Nigel Gv *ACOMB* YO24 23 F2
Nightingale Cl *HXB/STR* YO32 10 D5
Ninth Av *HEWTH* YO31 19 E4
Norfolk St *COP/BISH* YO23 24 A2
Norman Dr *RYKW* YO26 16 C3
Norman St *FUL/HES* YO10 25 E1
Norseway *STMFBR* YO41 15 F4
Northcote Av *ACOMB* YO24 23 E1
Northcroft *HXB/STR* YO32 7 E2
North Field La *COP/BISH* YO23 26 A1
RYKW YO26 16 A3
Northfields *HXB/STR* YO32 5 H1
Northlands Av *HXB/STR* YO32 7 F4
North La *ACOMB* YO24 23 E4
HXB/STR YO32 6 D2
HXB/STR YO32 11 F1
North Moor *HXB/STR* YO32 11 F2
Northmoor Cl *HXB/STR* YO32 11 E1
North Moor Gdns
HXB/STR YO32 11 E1
North Moor Rd *HXB/STR* YO32 11 E2
Northolme Dr *RAW/SKEL* YO30 9 F5
North Pde *RAW/SKEL* YO30 2 C2
North St *CYK* YO1 2 E4
Norway Dr *FUL/HES* YO10 24 B4
Nunmill St *COP/BISH* YO23 24 A2
Nunnery La *COP/BISH* YO23 2 D6
Nunthorpe Av *COP/BISH* YO23 23 H2
Nunthorpe Crs *COP/BISH* YO23 23 H2
Nunthorpe Dr *COP/BISH* YO23 24 A2
Nunthorpe Gdns
COP/BISH YO23 24 A2
Nunthorpe Gv *COP/BISH* YO23 23 H2
Nunthorpe Rd *ACOMB* YO24 2 D7
Nunthorpe Vw *COP/BISH* YO23 24 A3
Nursery Ct *RYKW* YO26 8 B4
Nursery Dr *ACOMB* YO24 23 E1
Nursery Gdns *FUL/HES* YO10 25 G1
Nursery Rd *RYKW* YO26 8 B4

O

Oakdale Rd *RAW/SKEL* YO30 9 G4
Oaken Gv *HXB/STR* YO32 6 C1
Oak Gld *HEWTH* YO31 11 E4
Oakhill Crs *HXB/STR* YO32 5 F4
Oakland Av *HEWTH* YO31 19 E2
Oakland Dr *HEWTH* YO31 19 F3
Oaklands *HXB/STR* YO32 5 G3
Oak Ri *ACOMB* YO24 22 C1
Oak St *RYKW* YO26 17 F4
Oak Tree Cl *HXB/STR* YO32 5 G3
Oak Tree Gv *HXB/STR* YO32 10 C4
Oak Tree La *HXB/STR* YO32 6 C4
Oak Tree Wy *HXB/STR* YO32 5 G3
Oakville St *HEWTH* YO31 18 C2
Ogleforth *CYK* YO1 3 F2
Old Brewery Gdns *TAD* LS24 31 E2
Old Coppice *HXB/STR* YO32 7 F2
Old Dike Lands *HXB/STR* YO32 6 C4
The Old Hwy *HXB/STR* YO32 5 G4
Oldman Ct *ACOMB* YO24 22 C4
Old Moor La *ACOMB* YO24 23 E5
Old Orch *HXB/STR* YO32 6 D3
The Old Orch *FUL/HES* YO10 24 C5
Old School Cl *FUL/HES* YO10 19 G5
Old School Ct *RYKW* YO26 8 A5
Old Station Yd *RYKS* YO19 * 21 H5
The Old Village *HXB/STR* YO32 11 E1
The Old Woodyard
STMFBR YO41 * 15 F3
Orchard Cottages *RYKS* YO19 21 H3
Orchard Gdns *HEWTH* YO31 10 D4
Orchard Garth *COP/BISH* YO23 26 D4
Orchard Paddock *HXB/STR* YO32 6 D3
Orchard Rd *RYKW* YO26 8 A5
The Orchard *FUL/HES* YO10 25 E3
Orchard Vw *RAW/SKEL* YO30 8 C1
Orchard Wy *ACOMB* YO24 23 E4
HXB/STR YO32 5 G2
Ordnance La *FUL/HES* YO10 24 B3
Oriel Gv *RAW/SKEL* YO30 17 H1
Orrin Cl *ACOMB* YO24 22 C5
Osbaldwick La *FUL/HES* YO10 19 H5
Osbaldwick Link Rd
FUL/HES YO10 20 A5
Osbaldwick Village
FUL/HES YO10 19 H5
Osbourne Dr *RAW/SKEL* YO30 9 F3
Osmington Gdns *HXB/STR* YO32 5 F3
Osprey Cl *ACOMB* YO24 22 B4

38 Ost - Sch

Ostler's Cl COP/BISH YO23 27 E4
Ostman Rd RYKW YO26 16 C4
Otterwood Bank ACOMB YO24 * 22 B3
Otterwood La ACOMB YO24 22 B3
Otterwood Paddock STMFBR YO41 15 E3
Ouse Acres RYKW YO26 17 E4
Ouse Br CYK YO1 2 E5
Ouseburn Av RYKW YO26 16 D3
Ousecliffe Gdns RAW/SKEL YO30 17 H3
Oust Lea RAW/SKEL YO30 17 G2
Ouston Cl TAD LS24 31 E3
Ouston La TAD LS24 31 E3
Outgang La HEWTH YO31 20 A3
Overdale Cl ACOMB YO24 22 D4
Ovington Ter COP/BISH YO23 23 H3
Owlwood Ct RYKS YO19 21 G4
Owlwood La RYKS YO19 21 G4
Owston Av FUL/HES YO10 25 E1
Ox Calder Cl RYKS YO19 21 H4
Ox Carr La HXB/STR YO32 5 G4
Ox Cl STMFBR YO41 15 G2
Oxford St ACOMB YO24 2 B7
Oxton Dr TAD LS24 31 E3
Oxton La TAD LS24 31 E3

P

Paddock Cha FUL/HES YO10 * 25 F3
Paddock Cl COP/BISH YO23 26 C5
HXB/STR YO32 11 E2
The Paddock RYKW YO26 16 D3
Paddock Wy RYKW YO26 16 D3
Palmer La CYK YO1 3 G4
Parade Ct HEWTH YO31 19 E3
Paragon St FUL/HES YO10 3 H7
Park Av HXB/STR YO32 10 C1
Park Cl RAW/SKEL YO30 8 C2
Park Crs HEWTH YO31 3 H1
Parker Av RYKW YO26 22 B2
Park Ga HXB/STR YO32 5 H1
Park Gv HEWTH YO31 18 C3
Parkland Dr TAD LS24 31 E2
Parkland Wy HXB/STR YO32 6 D3
Park La ACOMB YO24 23 F1
Park Ldg HXB/STR YO32 10 C2
Parkside Cl ACOMB YO24 23 E1
Park St ACOMB YO24 2 C7
Parliament St CYK YO1 3 F4
Paston Wk COP/BISH YO23 2 E7
Pasture Cl HXB/STR YO32 5 G4
RAW/SKEL YO30 8 C1
Pasture Farm Cl FUL/HES YO10 28 D1
Pasture La HEWTH YO31 19 G1
The Pastures ACOMB YO24 23 E4
Pately Pl RYKW YO26 17 E5
Patrick Pool CYK YO1 3 F4
Patterdale Dr RAW/SKEL YO30 9 F5
Pavement CYK YO1 3 F4
Paver La CYK YO1 3 H5
Pavilion Rw FUL/HES YO10 24 B5
Pear Tree Av RYKW YO26 8 A4
Pear Tree Cl HXB/STR YO32 11 E2
Pear Tree Ct CYK YO1 3 G3
Pear Tree La RYKS YO19 21 G4
Peasholme Gn CYK YO1 3 H4
Peckitt St CYK YO1 3 F6
Peel Cl FUL/HES YO10 25 E3
Peel St CYK YO1 3 H6
Pelham Pl HXB/STR YO32 5 F4
Pembroke St RAW/SKEL YO30 18 B2
Penleys Ct HEWTH YO31 * 3 G1
Penley's Grove St HEWTH YO31 3 G1
Pennine Cl HXB/STR YO32 11 E2
Penny Lane Ct CYK YO1 * 3 G3
Pentire Cl RAW/SKEL YO30 9 H5
Pentland Dr HXB/STR YO32 10 D3
Penyghent Av HEWTH YO31 19 F4
Peppercorn Cl RYKW YO26 17 F5
Percy's La CYK YO1 3 H5
Percy St HEWTH YO31 2 E2
Petercroft Cl RYKS YO19 21 H3
Petercroft La RYKS YO19 21 H3
Peter Hill Dr RAW/SKEL YO30 17 H1
Peter La CYK YO1 3 F4
Petersway RAW/SKEL YO30 18 A3
Pheasant Dr ACOMB YO24 22 B5
Philadelphia Ter COP/BISH YO23 23 H2
Phoenix Bvd RYKW YO26 2 A4
Piccadilly CYK YO1 3 G5
Pike Hills Mt COP/BISH YO23 26 C4
Pilgrim St HEWTH YO31 3 F1
Pinelands HXB/STR YO32 6 D4
Pinelands Wy FUL/HES YO10 25 G1
Pinewood Gv HEWTH YO31 10 D5
Pinewood Hl FUL/HES YO10 25 G1
Pinfold Ct RAW/SKEL YO30 17 H2
Pinsent Ct HEWTH YO31 18 D1
Plantation Dr RYKW YO26 16 D3
Plantation Gv RYKW YO26 16 D3
Plantation Wy HXB/STR YO32 6 B2
Ploughlands HXB/STR YO32 6 C4
Ploughman's Cl COP/BISH YO23 27 E4
Ploughmans' La HXB/STR YO32 6 C4
Plumer Av HEWTH YO31 19 F4
Pollard Cl HXB/STR YO32 10 D3
Poplar Gv HXB/STR YO32 10 D3
Poplar St RYKW YO26 17 F4
Poppleton Hall Gdn RYKW YO26 8 B3
Poppleton Rd RYKW YO26 17 F4
Portal Rd RYKW YO26 16 C2
Portisham Pl HXB/STR YO32 5 G4
Portland St HEWTH YO31 2 E2
Postern Cl COP/BISH YO23 3 F7
Potters Dr COP/BISH YO23 26 D4
Pottery La HEWTH YO31 18 D2
Precentor's Ct CYK YO1 2 E3
Prestwick Ct RYKW YO26 16 C4
Price's La COP/BISH YO23 2 E7
Primrose Vls RAW/SKEL YO30 18 A2
Princess Dr RYKW YO26 17 E3
Princess Rd HXB/STR YO32 5 G2
Prior's Wk RYKW YO26 17 E3
Priory St CYK YO1 2 D5
Priory Wood Wy HEWTH YO31 11 E4
Prospect Ct TAD LS24 30 D2
Prospect Dr TAD LS24 30 D2
Prospect Ter CYK YO1 2 D6
FUL/HES YO10 24 B5
Pulleyn Dr ACOMB YO24 23 F3

Q

Quaker Gn ACOMB YO24 22 C5
Quant Ms FUL/HES YO10 25 F1
Queen Anne's Rd RAW/SKEL YO30 2 C2
Queen's Gdns TAD LS24 30 C4
Queens Staith Ms CYK YO1 * 2 E6
Queen's Staith Rd CYK YO1 2 E5
Queen St ACOMB YO24 2 C6
Queenswood Gv ACOMB YO24 22 D2
Queen Victoria St COP/BISH YO23 23 H3

R

Racecourse Rd COP/BISH YO23 23 H4
Radley Ct HXB/STR YO32 5 F4
Railway Ter ACOMB YO24 2 A6
Railway Vw ACOMB YO24 23 E4
Rainsborough Wy RAW/SKEL YO30 17 H1
Ramsay Cl HEWTH YO31 18 C2
Ramsey Av COP/BISH YO23 28 A4
Ratcliffe Ct RAW/SKEL YO30 8 D1
Ratcliffe St RAW/SKEL YO30 18 A2
Raven Gv RYKW YO26 16 D5
Rawcliffe Av RAW/SKEL YO30 17 G1
Rawcliffe Cl RAW/SKEL YO30 9 F4
Rawcliffe Cft RAW/SKEL YO30 9 E4
Rawcliffe Dr RAW/SKEL YO30 17 G1
Rawcliffe Gv RAW/SKEL YO30 17 G2
Rawcliffe La RAW/SKEL YO30 17 G1
Rawcliffe Wy RAW/SKEL YO30 9 F4
Rawdon Av FUL/HES YO10 19 E5
Ray Dike Cl HXB/STR YO32 6 C4
Raynard Ct ACOMB YO24 * 22 C4
Rectory Gdns COP/BISH YO23 23 H3
Redbarn Dr FUL/HES YO10 25 H1
Redcoat Wy ACOMB YO24 22 B4
Redeness St HEWTH YO31 3 J3
Redgrave Cl HEWTH YO31 18 D1
Redman Cl FUL/HES YO10 24 A4
Redmayne Sq HXB/STR YO32 5 H1
Redmires Cl RAW/SKEL YO30 9 H5
Redthorn Dr HEWTH YO31 11 E5
Redwood Dr HXB/STR YO32 6 C2
The Reeves ACOMB YO24 22 C3
Regency Ms ACOMB YO24 23 F4
Regents Ct RYKW YO26 17 H4
Regents Ms RYKW YO26 17 E3
Regent St FUL/HES YO10 3 K7
Reginald Gv COP/BISH YO23 24 A3
Reighton Av RAW/SKEL YO30 17 G1
Reighton Dr RAW/SKEL YO30 9 G5
Renfrew Gn HXB/STR YO32 5 H1
Renshaw Gdns RYKW YO26 17 F5
Reygate Gv COP/BISH YO23 26 D5
Ribstone Gv HEWTH YO31 19 G3
Richardson St COP/BISH YO23 24 A2
Richmond St HEWTH YO31 3 J3
Ridgeway RYKW YO26 22 B1
Ringstone Rd RAW/SKEL YO30 9 G3
Ripley Gv HXB/STR YO32 6 C1
Risewood STMFBR YO41 14 B3
Rishworth Gv RAW/SKEL YO30 9 G5
Rivelin Wy RAW/SKEL YO30 9 G4
Riversdale HXB/STR YO32 7 F1
Riverside Crs HXB/STR YO32 7 F5
Riverside Gdns RYKW YO26 8 A4
Riverside Wk HXB/STR YO32 5 F3
RYKW YO26 8 A4
River St COP/BISH YO23 3 F7
Riversvale Dr RYKW YO26 8 A4
Robin Gv ACOMB YO24 23 F2
Robinson Dr ACOMB YO24 22 B2
Roche Av HEWTH YO31 18 D1
Rockcliff Ct TAD LS24 30 D2
Rockingham Av HEWTH YO31 19 F5
Rogers Ct ACOMB YO24 22 C4
Rolling Br TAD LS24 31 H1
Rolston Av HEWTH YO31 10 D4
Roman Av North STMFBR YO41 15 F3
Roman Av South STMFBR YO41 15 F4
Roman Cl TAD LS24 30 D2
Ropers Ct COP/BISH YO23 27 E4
The Ropewalk HEWTH YO31 3 J3
Roseberry Gv RAW/SKEL YO30 9 G3
Rosebery St RYKW YO26 17 G3
Rosecomb Wy HXB/STR YO32 6 D4
Rosecroft Wy RAW/SKEL YO30 17 F1
Rosedale Av RYKW YO26 16 D5
Rosedale St FUL/HES YO10 24 B2
Rosemary Ct CYK YO1 3 H5
TAD LS24 30 D2
Rosemary Pl CYK YO1 3 H5
Rosemary Rw TAD LS24 30 D2
Rose St HEWTH YO31 18 B2
Rose Tree Gv HXB/STR YO32 10 C2
Rosetta Wy RYKW YO26 17 E3
Rosslyn St RAW/SKEL YO30 17 H3
Rougier St CYK YO1 2 D4
Round Hl Link RAW/SKEL YO30 9 G4
Rowan Av HXB/STR YO32 10 C3
Rowan Pl HXB/STR YO32 10 C2
Rowley Ct HXB/STR YO32 7 F4
The Rowmans RAW/SKEL YO30 8 D2
Rowntree Av RAW/SKEL YO30 18 B1
Rowntree Whf CYK YO1 * 3 H5
Royal Cha ACOMB YO24 23 F4
Royston Cl HXB/STR YO32 5 H1
Ruby St COP/BISH YO23 23 H3
Rudcarr La RYKS YO19 13 F4
Ruddings Cl HXB/STR YO32 6 D3
Runswick Av RYKW YO26 16 C5
Rushwood Cl HXB/STR YO32 7 E2
Russel Dr RAW/SKEL YO30 17 F1
Russell St COP/BISH YO23 23 H2
Russet Dr HEWTH YO31 19 G4
Rutland Cl COP/BISH YO23 26 C4
Ryburn Cl RAW/SKEL YO30 9 G4
Rydal Av HEWTH YO31 19 F3
Rye Cl HXB/STR YO32 6 C3
Ryecroft HXB/STR YO32 5 F4
Ryecroft Av ACOMB YO24 22 C5
Ryecroft Cl HEWTH YO31 19 H1
Ryehill Cl HXB/STR YO32 10 C1
Ryemoor Rd HXB/STR YO32 6 C3
Rylatt Pl RYKW YO26 22 B1

S

Sadberge Ct FUL/HES YO10 25 G1
Saddlers Cl COP/BISH YO23 26 D4
HXB/STR YO32 11 E4
Sails Dr FUL/HES YO10 25 F1
St Aelreds Cl HEWTH YO31 19 E5
St Andrewgate CYK YO1 3 G3
St Andrew Pl CYK YO1 * 3 F4
St Andrews Ct CYK YO1 * 3 G3
St Ann's Ct FUL/HES YO10 24 B2
St Aubyn's Pl ACOMB YO24 23 G2
St Barnabas Cl RYKW YO26 17 G4
St Barnabas Ct RYKW YO26 * 17 G4
St Benedict Rd COP/BISH YO23 2 E7
St Benidict Rd COP/BISH YO23 2 E7
St Catherines Cl RAW/SKEL YO30 8 D1
St Catherines Pl ACOMB YO24 * 2 B7
St Chads Whf COP/BISH YO23 24 A4
St Clement's Gv COP/BISH YO23 24 A2
St Denys' Rd CYK YO1 3 G5
St Edmunds STMFBR YO41 15 G2
St Edward's Cl ACOMB YO24 23 F4
St George's Pl ACOMB YO24 23 F2
St Giles Ct HEWTH YO31 * 2 E2
St Giles Rd RAW/SKEL YO30 8
St Giles Wy COP/BISH YO23 26
St Helen's Rd ACOMB YO24 23
St Helen's Sq CYK YO1 2
St Hilda's Ms FUL/HES YO10 19
St James Cl RAW/SKEL YO30 9
St James Ct RYKW YO26 * 2
St James Mt COP/BISH YO23 23
St James Pl ACOMB YO24 22
St John's Crs HEWTH YO31 3
St John's Rd STMFBR YO41 15
St John St HEWTH YO31 3
St Josephs Ct ACOMB YO24 22
St Joseph's St TAD LS24 30
St Leonard's Pl RAW/SKEL YO30 2
St Luke's Gv RAW/SKEL YO30 18
St Margaret's Ter CYK YO1 3
St Mark's Gv RAW/SKEL YO30 9
St Martin's La CYK YO1 2
St Mary's RAW/SKEL YO30 2
St Mary's Cl HXB/STR YO32 5
HXB/STR YO32 6
St Mary's Gv FUL/HES YO10 19
St Marys Ms HXB/STR YO32 * 6
St Marys Sq CYK YO1 * 3
St Marys Ter RAW/SKEL YO30 * 2
St Maurice's Rd HEWTH YO31 3
St Michaels Ct ACOMB YO24 22
St Nicholas Av RYKS YO19 29
St Nicholas Cl COP/BISH YO23 26
St Nicholas Crs COP/BISH YO23 26
St Nicholas Pl FUL/HES YO10 * 24
St Nicholas Rd COP/BISH YO23 26
St Nicholas Wy HXB/STR YO32 6
St Olave's Rd RAW/SKEL YO30 2
St Oswald's Rd FUL/HES YO10 24
St Pauls Ms ACOMB YO24 2
St Paul's Sq ACOMB YO24 2
St Paul's Ter ACOMB YO24 2
St Peters Cl RYKW YO26 16
St Peters Ct RAW/SKEL YO30 * 18
St Peter's Gv RAW/SKEL YO30 2
St Philip's Gv RAW/SKEL YO30 17
St Sampson's Sq CYK YO1 3
St Saviourgate CYK YO1 3
St Saviour's Pl CYK YO1 3
St Stephens Ms RYKW YO26 22
St Stephen's Rd ACOMB YO24 22
St Stephen's Sq ACOMB YO24 22
St Swithin's Wk RYKW YO26 17
St Thomas' Pl HEWTH YO31 3
St Thomas's Cl FUL/HES YO10 19
St Wilfrid's Cl HXB/STR YO32 5
St Wilfrid's Rd HXB/STR YO32 5
St Wulstan Cl HEWTH YO31 18
Salisbury Rd RYKW YO26 17
Salisbury Ter RYKW YO26 17
Salmond Rd ACOMB YO24 22
Sandacre Ct RYKW YO26 17
Sandcroft Cl ACOMB YO24 22
Sandcroft Rd ACOMB YO24 22
Sanderson Ct RYKW YO26 22
Sandfield Ter TAD LS24 31
Sandholme HXB/STR YO32 7
Sandmartin Ct ACOMB YO24 22
Sandown Cl ACOMB YO24 23
Sandringham Cl HXB/STR YO32 6
Sandringham St FUL/HES YO10 24
Sandstock Rd HEWTH YO31 19
Sandy Gap HXB/STR YO32 6
Sandyland HXB/STR YO32 6
Sandy La HXB/STR YO32 6
HXB/STR YO32 13
Sandyridge RYKW YO26 8
Sargent Av COP/BISH YO23 27
Saville Gv RAW/SKEL YO30 17
Sawyer's Crs COP/BISH YO23 26
Sawyers Wk RYKS YO19 21
Saxford Wy HXB/STR YO32 6
Saxon Pl HEWTH YO31 18
Saxon Rd STMFBR YO41 15
Scafell Cl RAW/SKEL YO30 9
Scaife Gdns HEWTH YO31 18
Scaife Ms HEWTH YO31 * 18
Scaife St HEWTH YO31 18
Scarborough Ter RAW/SKEL YO30 18
Scarcroft Hl ACOMB YO24 23
Scarcroft La COP/BISH YO23 2
Scarcroft Rd ACOMB YO24 2
COP/BISH YO23 * 24
Scarcroft Vw COP/BISH YO23 2
Scaudercroft RYKS YO19 21
Scawton Av HEWTH YO31 10
School Cl STMFBR YO41 15
School La COP/BISH YO23 26
COP/BISH YO23 28
FUL/HES YO10 24
FUL/HES YO10 25

Sch – Wes 39

ool St ACOMB YO24 ... 22 D1
reby La STMFBR YO41 ... 14 C4
tt Moncrieff Rd
XB/STR YO32 ... 5 H4
tt St COP/BISH YO23 ... 24 A2
ven Gv HXB/STR YO32 ... 7 E2
ope Av HEWTH YO31 ... 3 K2
fire Cl RAW/SKEL YO30 ... 9 H3
ton Cl FUL/HES YO10 ... 19 H5
ond Av HEWTH YO31 ... 19 E3
ge Ri TAD LS24 ... 30 A4
ton Av HEWTH YO31 ... 19 E1
rave Wk RYKW YO26 ... 17 F5
oy Rd RYKS YO19 ... 29 E2
don Rd RYKW YO26 ... 17 F4
enth Av HEWTH YO31 ... 19 E4
ern Gn RYKW YO26 ... 16 D1
erus Av ACOMB YO24 ... 17 E5
erus St ACOMB YO24 ... 22 D1
mour Gv HEWTH YO31 ... 19 E3
llowdale Gv FUL/HES YO10 ... 19 H5
mbles CYK YO1 ... 3 F4
w's Ter ACOMB YO24 ... 2 C7
lley Dr HXB/STR YO32 ... 5 F3
lley Gv RAW/SKEL YO30 ... 17 F1
rbourne Gv HXB/STR YO32 ... 5 G3
rringham Dr ACOMB YO24 ... 22 D4
rwood Gv HEWTH YO31 ... 11 E5
YKW YO26 ... 16 C3
ton Garth Cl HXB/STR YO32 ... 7 F4
oton Rd RAW/SKEL YO30 ... 8 D2
oton St RAW/SKEL YO30 ... 18 B2
ley Av RYKW YO26 ... 16 D3
tel Cl RAW/SKEL YO30 ... 17 G1
erdale Ct ACOMB YO24 ... 22 D5
er St CYK YO1 ... 3 F4
Balk La COP/BISH YO23 ... 27 G2
mons Cl HXB/STR YO32 ... 5 F3
cco Ct HEWTH YO31 ... 18 C1
vell Gv RYKW YO26 ... 16 D4
ard St FUL/HES YO10 ... 25 E1
h Av HEWTH YO31 ... 3 K2
ldergate CYK YO1 ... 2 E6
ldergate Br COP/BISH YO23 ... 3 F6
lton Br RYKW YO26 ... 8 B3
lton Ct RAW/SKEL YO30 ... 17 H3
wsby Gv HEWTH YO31 ... 11 E5
ddaw ACOMB YO24 ... 22 C5
ssor Rd ACOMB YO24 ... 22 B3
e La TAD LS24 ... 31 H3
gsby Gv ACOMB YO24 ... 23 E4
ales' St CYK YO1 ... 2 E6
ary La RYKS YO19 ... 20 D3
eaton Gv RYKW YO26 ... 16 D4
ith Cl FUL/HES YO10 ... 24 D4
ithie Cl HXB/STR YO32 ... 10 C1
nerset Cl RAW/SKEL YO30 ... 9 F3
nerset Rd HEWTH YO31 ... 18 C1
th Bank Av COP/BISH YO23 ... 23 H3
th Down Rd HXB/STR YO32 ... 11 E1
th Esp CYK YO1 ... 3 F6
thfield Crs ACOMB YO24 ... 23 E4
thfields Rd HXB/STR YO32 ... 5 G2
thlands HXB/STR YO32 ... 6 C1
thlands Rd COP/BISH YO23 ... 23 H2
th La HXB/STR YO32 ... 6 D2
tholme Dr RAW/SKEL YO30 ... 17 G1
th Pde ACOMB YO24 ... 2 C6
th Pk ACOMB YO24 * ... 22 C3
verby Rd RYKW YO26 ... 17 E5
lding Av RAW/SKEL YO30 ... 17 H2
culation St CYK YO1 ... 3 J5
ncer St COP/BISH YO23 ... 2 E7
n La CYK YO1 ... 3 G3
y Bank ACOMB YO24 ... 27 E1
ndle Cl ACOMB YO24 ... 22 C4
Spinney ACOMB YO24 ... 23 F5
ingbank Av RYKS YO19 ... 21 G3
ingfield Cl HEWTH YO31 ... 19 G2
ingfield Rd RYKW YO26 ... 8 A4
ingfield Wy HEWTH YO31 ... 19 G2
inghill Ct TAD LS24 ... 30 D2
ing La FUL/HES YO10 ... 25 E3
ingwood HXB/STR YO32 ... 6 D4
ingwood Gv RYKW YO26 ... 16 D3
uce Cl HXB/STR YO32 ... 10 C4
rriergate CYK YO1 ... 3 F5
Square STMFBR YO41 ... 15 F2
AD LS24 ... 31 E2
bler Cl HXB/STR YO32 ... 6 A2
blers Wk HXB/STR YO32 * ... 7 F4
Stables FUL/HES YO10 * ... 24 B3
indale Cl RAW/SKEL YO30 ... 9 F4
thes Cl RYKW YO26 ... 16 D5
nford Br West
TMFBR YO41 ... 15 E2
nford St East RYKW YO26 ... 17 G4
nford St West RYKW YO26 * ... 17 F4
nley Av HXB/STR YO32 ... 6 D4
Stanley St HEWTH YO31 ... 18 C2
Starkey Crs HEWTH YO31 ... 19 F4
Station Av CYK YO1 ... 2 D4
HXB/STR YO32 ... 10 C3
Station Est TAD LS24 * ... 30 C3
Station Ri CYK YO1 ... 2 D4
Station Rd ACOMB YO24 ... 2 C5
COP/BISH YO23 ... 26 C5
HXB/STR YO32 ... 7 E2
RYKW YO26 ... 16 A1
TAD LS24 ... 30 C3
Station Sq HXB/STR YO32 ... 5 G3
Steeple Cl HXB/STR YO32 ... 6 B2
Stephenson Cl HXB/STR YO32 ... 10 D5
Stephenson Wy RYKW YO26 ... 17 G4
Sterne Av HEWTH YO31 ... 19 F4
Stirling Gv FUL/HES YO10 ... 24 D4
Stirling Rd RAW/SKEL YO30 ... 9 H3
Stirrup Cl ACOMB YO24 ... 22 B4
Stockhill Cl RYKS YO19 ... 21 G3
Stockholm Cl FUL/HES YO10 ... 24 A4
Stockton La HEWTH YO31 ... 19 F2
The Stonebow CYK YO1 ... 3 G4
Stone Br FUL/HES YO10 ... 29 E1
Stonegate CYK YO1 ... 2 E4
Stonegate Wk CYK YO1 * ... 2 E3
Stonelands Ct
RAW/SKEL YO30 ... 9 H5
Stone Riggs HXB/STR YO32 ... 12 D2
Stonethwaite ACOMB YO24 ... 22 C5
Stonewall Cottage La
STMFBR YO41 ... 15 F3
Stoop Cl HXB/STR YO32 ... 6 C3
Stow Ct HXB/STR YO32 ... 10 D3
Straight La RYKS YO19 ... 21 H1
Stratford Wy HXB/STR YO32 ... 10 D3
HXB/STR YO32 ... 11 E3
Stray Garth HEWTH YO31 ... 19 E2
Straylands Gv HEWTH YO31 ... 19 E1
Stray Rd HEWTH YO31 ... 19 G3
Strensall New Br
HXB/STR YO32 ... 5 E2
Strensall Pk HXB/STR YO32 ... 7 H1
Strensall Rd HXB/STR YO32 ... 11 E1
Stripe La RAW/SKEL YO30 ... 8 C1
Stuart Rd ACOMB YO24 ... 22 D3
Stubden Gv RAW/SKEL YO30 ... 9 G4
Sturdee Gv HEWTH YO31 ... 18 D2
Summerfield Rd ACOMB YO24 ... 22 C5
Sunningdale Cl RYKW YO26 ... 16 C4
Sunnydale HXB/STR YO32 ... 6 D4
Surrey Wy RAW/SKEL YO30 ... 17 G1
Surtees St RAW/SKEL YO30 ... 18 A2
Sussex Cl FUL/HES YO10 ... 25 G2
Sussex Rd FUL/HES YO10 ... 25 G2
Sussex Wy HXB/STR YO32 ... 5 F4
Sutherland St COP/BISH YO23 ... 23 H3
Sutor Cl COP/BISH YO23 ... 26 D4
Sutton Wy RAW/SKEL YO30 ... 18 A1
Swale Av ACOMB YO24 ... 23 E4
Swann St COP/BISH YO23 ... 2 D7
Swards Wy FUL/HES YO10 ... 25 E2
Swarthdale HXB/STR YO32 ... 7 E1
Swinegate CYK YO1 ... 3 F4
Swinegate Ct East CYK YO1 * ... 3 F3
Swinerton Av RYKW YO26 ... 17 G3
Swinsty Ct RAW/SKEL YO30 ... 9 G5
Sycamore Av HXB/STR YO32 ... 10 C2
Sycamore Cl HXB/STR YO32 ... 6 D4
RAW/SKEL YO30 ... 8 D1
Sycamore Pl RAW/SKEL YO30 ... 2 C2
Sycamore Ter RAW/SKEL YO30 ... 2 C3
Sycamore Vw RYKW YO26 ... 8 A5
Sykes Cl RAW/SKEL YO30 * ... 18 A3

T

Tadcaster Rd ACOMB YO24 ... 23 G3
COP/BISH YO23 ... 26 D3
Tadcaster Rd Dringhouses
ACOMB YO24 ... 23 E5
Tamworth Rd RAW/SKEL YO30 ... 9 H5
Tang Hall La FUL/HES YO10 ... 19 G5
Tanner Rw CYK YO1 ... 2 D5
Tanner St CYK YO1 ... 2 D4
The Tannery FUL/HES YO10 ... 3 J6
Tarbert Crs ACOMB YO24 ... 22 B5
Tatton Cl RAW/SKEL YO30 ... 10 A5
Taylors Cl RYKS YO19 ... 13 H5
Teal Dr ACOMB YO24 ... 22 C4
Teck St COP/BISH YO23 * ... 24 A2
Tedder Rd ACOMB YO24 ... 22 B3
Telford Ter COP/BISH YO23 ... 23 H2
Templars Ct COP/BISH YO23 * ... 26 C5
Temple Av FUL/HES YO10 ... 19 G5
Templemead HEWTH YO31 ... 18 D1
Temple Rd COP/BISH YO23 ... 27 H3
Tennent Rd ACOMB YO24 ... 22 B2
Tennyson Av RAW/SKEL YO30 ... 18 B2
Ten Thorn La RYKW YO26 ... 16 B5
Terrington Cl HXB/STR YO32 ... 5 G1
Terry Av COP/BISH YO23 ... 3 F7
FUL/HES YO10 ... 24 A3
Terry St COP/BISH YO23 ... 24 A3
Thanet Rd ACOMB YO24 ... 22 D3
Thatchers Cft COP/BISH YO23 ... 26 D4
Theresa Cl HXB/STR YO32 ... 11 E5
Thief La FUL/HES YO10 ... 24 D1
FUL/HES YO10 ... 25 E1
Third Av HEWTH YO31 ... 19 E4
Thirkleby Wy FUL/HES YO10 ... 19 H5
Thirlmere Dr HEWTH YO31 ... 19 F3
Thomas St FUL/HES YO10 ... 3 K6
Thompson Pl RYKW YO26 ... 17 F4
Thoresby Rd ACOMB YO24 ... 22 B3
Thornbeck RYKS YO19 ... 21 G5
Thorncroft RYKS YO19 ... 21 H3
Thornfield Av HEWTH YO31 ... 19 E1
Thornfield Dr HEWTH YO31 ... 10 D4
Thornhills HXB/STR YO32 ... 7 F2
Thorn Nook HEWTH YO31 ... 19 E1
Thornton Moor Cl
RAW/SKEL YO30 ... 9 G4
Thorntree Gv
RAW/SKEL YO30 ... 10 A4
Thornwood Covert
ACOMB YO24 ... 22 C3
Thorpe St COP/BISH YO23 ... 23 H2
Tilmire Cl FUL/HES YO10 ... 24 D4
Tisbury Rd RYKW YO26 ... 17 F5
Tithe Cl ACOMB YO24 ... 22 B3
Toby Ct HXB/STR YO32 ... 5 F3
Toft Gn CYK YO1 ... 2 D5
Toll Bar Wy TAD LS24 ... 31 F1
Top La COP/BISH YO23 ... 26 C4
Toremill Cl HXB/STR YO32 ... 10 C2
Torridon Pl ACOMB YO24 ... 22 B5
Tostig Av RYKW YO26 ... 16 D4
Tostig Cl STMFBR YO41 ... 15 F3
Tower Crs TAD LS24 ... 30 B2
Tower Pl CYK YO1 * ... 3 F6
Tower St CYK YO1 ... 3 F6
Town End Gdns HXB/STR YO32 ... 6 B1
Towthorpe Br HXB/STR YO32 ... 5 E5
Towthorpe Moor La
HXB/STR YO32 ... 7 H1
Towthorpe Rd HXB/STR YO32 ... 7 E2
Towton Av ACOMB YO24 ... 23 F2
Trafalgar St COP/BISH YO23 ... 23 H3
Tranby Av RYKS YO19 ... 20 A5
Trans Pennine Trail
COP/BISH YO23 ... 27 H2
Trenchard Rd RYKW YO26 ... 16 C3
Trenfield Ct ACOMB YO24 * ... 23 F1
Trent Av HXB/STR YO32 ... 7 F5
Trentholme Dr ACOMB YO24 ... 23 G2
Trent Wy ACOMB YO24 ... 22 D5
Trevor Gv ACOMB YO24 ... 23 F2
Tribune Wy RAW/SKEL YO30 ... 9 H4
Trinity Ct CYK YO1 * ... 2 D5
Trinity La CYK YO1 ... 2 D5
Trinity Mdw HXB/STR YO32 ... 13 E1
Troon Cl RYKW YO26 ... 16 C4
Troutbeck ACOMB YO24 ... 22 C5
Troutsdale Av RAW/SKEL YO30 ... 9 F4
Tudor Rd ACOMB YO24 ... 22 D2
Tuke Av FUL/HES YO10 ... 19 G5
Turks Head Ct CYK YO1 * ... 3 F3
Turnberry Dr RYKW YO26 ... 16 C5
Turner's Cft FUL/HES YO10 ... 25 F4
Turnmire Rd ACOMB YO24 ... 23 E4
Turnpike Rd TAD LS24 ... 31 F1
Turpin Ct CYK YO1 * ... 3 G6
Twin Pike Wy HXB/STR YO32 ... 6 B2
Tyneham Wy HXB/STR YO32 ... 5 G3

U

Ullswater ACOMB YO24 ... 22 C5
Undercroft RYKS YO19 ... 21 H3
Union Ter HEWTH YO31 ... 3 F1
University Rd FUL/HES YO10 ... 25 E2
Uppercroft HXB/STR YO32 ... 6 C2
Upper Hanover St
RYKW YO26 * ... 17 G4
Upper Newborough St
RAW/SKEL YO30 ... 18 B2
Upper Price St
COP/BISH YO23 ... 23 H2
Upper St Paul's Ter
ACOMB YO24 ... 2 A5
RYKW YO26 ... 16 C5
Usher La HXB/STR YO32 ... 7 E2
Usher Park Rd HXB/STR YO32 ... 7 E1

V

The Vale RAW/SKEL YO30 ... 8 C1
Vanbrugh Dr FUL/HES YO10 ... 25 G1
Vanbrugh Wy FUL/HES YO10 ... 25 E2
Varvills Ct CYK YO1 * ... 2 D5
Vavasour Ct COP/BISH YO23 ... 26 D5
Vernon Cl COP/BISH YO23 ... 28 A4
Vernon Rd RAW/SKEL YO30 ... 9 F4
Vesper Dr ACOMB YO24 ... 22 B2
Vesper Wk HXB/STR YO32 ... 7 F5
Vicarage Gdns FUL/HES YO10 ... 19 H5
Vicars Cl COP/BISH YO23 ... 26 D5
Victoria Ct RYKW YO26 ... 17 G4
Victoria Wy HXB/STR YO32 ... 10 D5
Victor St CYK YO1 ... 2 E6
Viking Cl STMFBR YO41 ... 15 F3
Viking Rd RYKW YO26 ... 16 D4
STMFBR YO41 ... 15 F3
Village Garth HXB/STR YO32 ... 6 C1
Village St RAW/SKEL YO30 ... 9 F3
The Village HXB/STR YO32 ... 5 G2
HXB/STR YO32 ... 6 C1
HXB/STR YO32 ... 13 E2
Villa Gv HEWTH YO31 ... 3 J1
Vincent Wy ACOMB YO24 ... 22 C4
Vine St COP/BISH YO23 ... 24 A2
Vyner St HEWTH YO31 ... 18 B2

W

Waggoners Dr COP/BISH YO23 ... 26 D4
Waincroft HXB/STR YO32 ... 5 F4
Wainers Cl COP/BISH YO23 ... 26 D4
Wain's Gv ACOMB YO24 ... 22 D5
Wain's Rd ACOMB YO24 ... 22 D4
Walker Dr ACOMB YO24 ... 22 B4
Walmer Carr HXB/STR YO32 ... 6 A2
Walmgate CYK YO1 ... 3 H6
Walney Rd HEWTH YO31 ... 19 F4
Walnut Cl FUL/HES YO10 ... 25 E3
HXB/STR YO32 ... 6 D2
Walpole St HEWTH YO31 ... 18 C2
Walton Pl RYKW YO26 ... 22 B2
Walworth St North
RYKW YO26 ... 17 G4
Walworth St South
RYKW YO26 * ... 17 G4
Wandhill HXB/STR YO32 ... 6 C2
The Wandle RYKW YO26 ... 22 A2
Wansbeck ACOMB YO24 ... 26 D1
Warwick St HEWTH YO31 ... 18 C2
Wasdale Cl RAW/SKEL YO30 ... 9 F5
Waterdale Pk HEWTH YO31 ... 10 D5
Water End RYKW YO26 ... 17 G3
Waterings HXB/STR YO32 ... 6 B2
Water La RAW/SKEL YO30 ... 9 H4
RYKS YO19 ... 21 H3
Waterman Ct ACOMB YO24 ... 22 B3
Watson St ACOMB YO24 ... 2 A7
Watson Ter ACOMB YO24 ... 2 A6
Wattlers Cl COP/BISH YO23 ... 26 D4
Waveney Gv RAW/SKEL YO30 ... 18 A1
Waverley St HEWTH YO31 ... 3 G2
Waynefleet Gv FUL/HES YO10 ... 25 E1
Weavers Cl COP/BISH YO23 ... 26 D4
Weavers Pk COP/BISH YO23 ... 26 D4
Weddall Cl ACOMB YO24 ... 23 F3
Welborn Cl FUL/HES YO10 ... 19 F5
Welland Ri RYKW YO26 ... 17 E4
Wellesley Cl RAW/SKEL YO30 ... 9 H4
Wellington Rw CYK YO1 ... 2 D4
Wellington St FUL/HES YO10 ... 3 J7
Welton Av RYKW YO26 ... 17 E4
Welwyn Dr FUL/HES YO10 ... 24 C4
Wenham Rd ACOMB YO24 ... 22 C4
Wenlock Ter FUL/HES YO10 ... 24 B3
Wensleydale Dr FUL/HES YO10 ... 20 A5
Wentworth Rd ACOMB YO24 ... 23 H2
Wentworth Wy FUL/HES YO10 ... 24 D2
The Werkdyke CYK YO1 * ... 3 G3
West Bank ACOMB YO24 ... 23 E1
West End HXB/STR YO32 ... 5 F2
West End Cl HXB/STR YO32 ... 5 G2
Westerdale Ct RAW/SKEL YO30 ... 17 H3
Westfield Cl HXB/STR YO32 ... 6 C2
Westfield Ct COP/BISH YO23 ... 26 C5
Westfield Crs TAD LS24 ... 30 C3
Westfield Dr FUL/HES YO10 ... 24 B4
Westfield Gv HXB/STR YO32 ... 6 B2
Westfield La HXB/STR YO32 ... 6 B2
Westfield Pl ACOMB YO24 ... 22 B3
HXB/STR YO32 ... 6 C2
Westfield Rd HXB/STR YO32 ... 6 C2
Westfield Sq TAD LS24 ... 30 C2

40 Wes - Yor

Westfield Ter *TAD* LS24 .... 30 C2
Westgate *TAD* LS24 .... 30 C3
Westholme Dr *RAW/SKEL* YO30 .... 9 F5
Westlands Gv *HEWTH* YO31 .... 19 E2
Westminster Rd
RAW/SKEL YO30 .... 17 H3
West Moor La *FUL/HES* YO10 .... 25 F4
West Mt *TAD* LS24 .... 30 B4
West Nooks *HXB/STR* YO32 .... 7 F2
Westpit La *HXB/STR* YO32 .... 5 F3
West Thorpe *ACOMB* YO24 .... 22 D4
Westview Cl *RYKW* YO26 .... 16 C2
Westwood Ms *RYKS* YO19 .... 21 H3
Westwood Ter *COP/BISH* YO23 .... 23 H3
Wetherby Rd *RYKW* YO26 .... 22 A1
TAD LS24 .... 30 B2
Wharfe Dr *ACOMB* YO24 .... 22 D4
Wharnscliffe Dr *RAW/SKEL* YO30 .... 9 G4
Wharton Av *RAW/SKEL* YO30 .... 18 A2
Wharton Cl *STMFBR* YO41 .... 15 G2
Wharton Rd *STMFBR* YO41 .... 15 G2
Wheatcroft *HXB/STR* YO32 .... 5 F4
Wheatfield La *HXB/STR* YO32 .... 6 D3
Wheatlands Gv *RYKW* YO26 .... 16 D3
Wheatley Dr *HXB/STR* YO32 .... 6 C3
Wheeldale Dr *HXB/STR* YO32 .... 12 B4
The Wheelhouse
RAW/SKEL YO30 .... 8 C1
Wheelwright Cl *COP/BISH* YO23 .... 26 D4
Wheldrake La *RYKS* YO19 .... 29 H5
Whenby Gv *HEWTH* YO31 .... 11 E5
Whernside Av *HEWTH* YO31 .... 19 F4
Whin Cl *ACOMB* YO24 .... 23 F5
HXB/STR YO32 .... 5 G4
Whin Garth *ACOMB* YO24 .... 23 F5
Whin Rd *ACOMB* YO24 .... 27 H1
Whip-Ma-Whop-Ma-Ga *CYK* YO1 .... 3 G4
Whistler Cl *COP/BISH* YO23 .... 27 E4
Whitby Av *HEWTH* YO31 .... 19 F2
Whitby Dr *HEWTH* YO31 .... 19 F2
Whitecross Gdns *HEWTH* YO31 .... 18 C2
White Cross Rd *HEWTH* YO31 .... 18 C2
White Horse Cl *HXB/STR* YO32 .... 11 E1
White House Dl *ACOMB* YO24 .... 23 F2
White House Dr *ACOMB* YO24 .... 23 F2
White House Gdns
ACOMB YO24 .... 23 F3
White House Ri *ACOMB* YO24 .... 23 F3
Whitelands *HXB/STR* YO32 .... 7 F3
White Rose Av *HXB/STR* YO32 .... 10 C3
White Rose Cl *RYKW* YO26 .... 8 C5
Whiterose Dr *STMFBR* YO41 .... 15 G3
White Rose Gv *HXB/STR* YO32 .... 10 C3
White Rose Wy *RYKW* YO26 .... 16 C1
Whitestone Dr *HEWTH* YO31 .... 10 D4
Whitethorn Cl *HEWTH* YO31 .... 10 D4
Whitley Cl *RAW/SKEL* YO30 .... 9 H5
Whitton Pl *FUL/HES* YO10 .... 19 H5
Wigginton Rd *HEWTH* YO31 .... 18 B2
Wigginton Ter *HEWTH* YO31 .... 18 B2
Wighill Garth *TAD* LS24 .... 30 D2
Wighill La *TAD* LS24 .... 30 D2
Wilberforce Av *RAW/SKEL* YO30 .... 18 A2
Wilkinson Wy *HXB/STR* YO32 .... 5 F2
William Plows Av
FUL/HES YO10 .... 24 C2
Willis St *FUL/HES* YO10 .... 3 J7
Willoughby Wy *ACOMB* YO24 .... 22 B4
Willow Bank *HXB/STR* YO32 .... 10 D3
Willow Ct *STMFBR* YO41 .... 15 E3
Willow Gld *HXB/STR* YO32 .... 11 E3
Willow Gv *HEWTH* YO31 .... 19 E2
HXB/STR YO32 .... 7 G4
Willow Ri *TAD* LS24 .... 30 B4
The Willows *HXB/STR* YO32 .... 5 G3
RAW/SKEL YO30 * 18 A2
Wilsthorpe Gv *FUL/HES* YO10 .... 24 D4
Wilstrop Farm Rd
COP/BISH YO23 .... 26 C5
Wilton Ri *ACOMB* YO24 .... 23 F1
Wimpole Cl *RAW/SKEL* YO30 .... 9 H5
Winchester Av *RYKW* YO26 .... 17 F5
Winchester Gv *RYKW* YO26 .... 17 F5
Windermere *ACOMB* YO24 .... 22 D5
Windmill Gv *TAD* LS24 .... 30 B4
Windmill La *FUL/HES* YO10 .... 25 F1
Windmill Ri *RYKW* YO26 .... 23 E1
TAD LS24 .... 30 B5
Windmill Wy *HXB/STR* YO32 .... 7 E2
Windsor Dr *HXB/STR* YO32 .... 6 A1
Windsor Garth *ACOMB* YO24 .... 22 D3
Windsor St *COP/BISH* YO23 .... 23 H3
Winscar Gv *RAW/SKEL* YO30 .... 9 F4
Winterscale Ct *FUL/HES* YO10 * 24 B2
Winterscale St *FUL/HES* YO10 .... 24 B2
Witham Dr *HXB/STR* YO32 .... 7 G5
Woburn Cl *HXB/STR* YO32 .... 5 H1
Wolfe Av *HEWTH* YO31 .... 19 E4
Wolsey Dr *COP/BISH* YO23 .... 28 A4
Wolsley St *FUL/HES* YO10 .... 3 J7
Wolviston Av *FUL/HES* YO10 .... 25 G1
Wood Cl *HXB/STR* YO32 .... 5 F3
Woodcock Cl *HXB/STR* YO32 .... 7 E2
Woodford Pl *ACOMB* YO24 .... 22 D3
Woodhouse Gv *HEWTH* YO31 .... 19 F4
Woodland Cha *RAW/SKEL* YO30 .... 10 A5
Woodland Pl *HXB/STR* YO32 .... 10 D2
Woodlands Av *HXB/STR* YO32 .... 6 C3
TAD LS24 .... 30 A4
Woodlands Gv *HEWTH* YO31 .... 19 F1
Woodlands Vw *TAD* LS24 .... 30 B4
Woodland Wy *HXB/STR* YO32 .... 11 E2
Woodlea Av *RYKW* YO26 .... 16 D5
Woodlea Bank *RYKW* YO26 .... 16 D5
Woodlea Crs *RYKW* YO26 16
Woodlea Gv *RYKW* YO26 16
Woodleigh Cl *HXB/STR* YO32 5
Woodside Av *HEWTH* YO31 19
Wood St *HEWTH* YO31 3
Wood Wy *HXB/STR* YO32 11
Woolnough Av *FUL/HES* YO10 25
Worcester Dr *HEWTH* YO31 19
Wordsworth Crs *ACOMB* YO24 22
Wray's Av *HEWTH* YO31 10
Wycliffe Av *FUL/HES* YO10 19
Wydale Rd *FUL/HES* YO10 20
Wykeham Rd *RYKW* YO26 16
Wyre Ct *HXB/STR* YO32 * 6

Y

Yarburgh Gv *RYKW* YO26 17
Yarburgh Wy *FUL/HES* YO10 25
Yearsley Crs *HEWTH* YO31 18
Yearsley Gv *HEWTH* YO31 10
Yew Tree Ms *FUL/HES* YO10 19
York Rd *ACOMB* YO24 22
HXB/STR YO32 6
RYKS YO19 21
TAD LS24 31
York & Selby Pth
COP/BISH YO23 24
COP/BISH YO23 27
CYK YO1 2
RAW/SKEL YO30 8
RYKW YO26 2
York & Selby Pth & Trans Penine Trail
COP/BISH YO23 28
York St *RYKS* YO19 21

Index - featured places

1066 Battlesite
STMFBR YO41 .... 15 H3
Aaron Rd Industrial Estate
HEWTH YO31 .... 18 D1
Acomb Primary School
ACOMB YO24 .... 23 E1
Acomb Wood Shopping Centre
ACOMB YO24 .... 22 B5
Acorn Business Centre
FUL/HES YO10 .... 3 J6
Alhambra Court Hotel
RAW/SKEL YO30 .... 2 D2
Allied Leisure Megabowl
RAW/SKEL YO30 .... 9 H2
All Saints RC Lower School
COP/BISH YO23 .... 2 D6
All Saints RC Upper School
COP/BISH YO23 .... 23 G2
Applefields School
HEWTH YO31 .... 19 G4
Archbishop Holgates School
FUL/HES YO10 .... 25 G1
Archbishop of York CE Junior School
COP/BISH YO23 .... 27 H3
The ARC
CYK YO1 .... 3 G4
Askham Bryan College of Agriculture & Horticulture
COP/BISH YO23 .... 26 A4
Assembly Rooms
CYK YO1 .... 2 E3
Badger Hill Primary School
FUL/HES YO10 .... 25 F2
Barbican Leisure Centre
FUL/HES YO10 .... 3 H7
The Bar Convent Museum
ACOMB YO24 .... 2 D6
Barfield Estate
HXB/STR YO32 .... 11 F5
Barley Hall
CYK YO1 .... 3 F3
Bedern Hall
CYK YO1 .... 3 G3
Beechwood Close Hotel
RAW/SKEL YO30 .... 17 G2
Best Western Kilima Hotel
ACOMB YO24 .... 23 F1
Best Western Monkbar Hotel
HEWTH YO31 .... 3 G2
Best Western York Pavilion Hotel
FUL/HES YO10 .... 24 C5
Bishopthorpe Infant School
COP/BISH YO23 .... 28 A3
Blue Bridge Hotel
FUL/HES YO10 .... 3 G7
Bootham Bar
RAW/SKEL YO30 .... 2 E2
Bootham School
RAW/SKEL YO30 .... 2 D2
Burnholme Community College
HEWTH YO31 .... 19 F4
Burton Green Primary School
RAW/SKEL YO30 .... 18 A1
Canon Lee School
RAW/SKEL YO30 .... 17 H1
Carr J & I School
RYKW YO26 .... 16 D4
The Chien Clinic
ACOMB YO24 .... 23 F3
City Screen
CYK YO1 .... 2 E4
Clementhorpe Health Centre
COP/BISH YO23 .... 24 A2
Clifford's Tower
CYK YO1 .... 3 F6
Clifton Bridge Hotel
RAW/SKEL YO30 .... 17 H3
Clifton Green Primary School
RAW/SKEL YO30 .... 18 A2
Clifton Health Centre
RAW/SKEL YO30 .... 17 H2
Clifton Moor Business Village
RAW/SKEL YO30 .... 9 G4
Clifton Preparatory School
RAW/SKEL YO30 .... 2 B1
Clifton Without Junior School
RAW/SKEL YO30 .... 17 G1
Compass Drug Dependency Clinic
ACOMB YO24 .... 2 B7
Copmanthorpe Primary School
COP/BISH YO23 .... 26 D4
Coppergate Walk Shopping Centre
CYK YO1 .... 3 G5
Dean Court Hotel
CYK YO1 .... 2 E3
The Deanery
CYK YO1 .... 3 F2
Derwent Junior School
FUL/HES YO10 .... 19 G5
Derwent Valley Industrial Estate
RYKS YO19 .... 21 H5
Dick Turpin's Grave
CYK YO1 .... 3 G6
DIG
CYK YO1 .... 3 G4
Dringhouses Primary School
ACOMB YO24 .... 23 E4
Dunnington Primary School
RYKS YO19 .... 21 F3
Ebor Industrial Estate
HEWTH YO31 .... 3 K3
Ebor School
RAW/SKEL YO30 .... 17 H3
Edmund Wilson Swimming Baths
ACOMB YO24 .... 22 D3
English Martyrs RC Primary School
ACOMB YO24 .... 23 F1
Fairfax House
CYK YO1 .... 3 F5
Fishergate Bar
CYK YO1 .... 3 G6
Fishergate Postern
FUL/HES YO10 .... 3 G6
Fishergate Primary School
FUL/HES YO10 .... 3 H7
Forest Park Golf Club
HXB/STR YO32 .... 12 D2
Fulford Golf Club
FUL/HES YO10 .... 25 E4
Fulford Industrial Estate
FUL/HES YO10 .... 24 A3
Fulford School
FUL/HES YO10 .... 24 C5
Grand Opera House
CYK YO1 .... 2 E5
The Grange Hotel
RAW/SKEL YO30 .... 2 C1
Green Lane Trading Estate
RAW/SKEL YO30 .... 9 H5
Haxby Road Primary School
HEWTH YO31 .... 18 C2
Haxby Shopping Centre
HXB/STR YO32 .... 6 D2
Haxby & Wigginton Health Centre
HXB/STR YO32 .... 6 C2
Headlands Primary School
HXB/STR YO32 .... 6 C3
Hempland Primary School
HEWTH YO31 .... 19 G3
Heworth CE Primary School
HEWTH YO31 .... 19 E3
Heworth CC & York Hockey Club
HEWTH YO31 19
Hob Moor Primary School & Hob Moor Oaks School
ACOMB YO24 22
The Hospitium
RAW/SKEL YO30 2
Hull & York Medical School
FUL/HES YO10 25
Huntington Primary School
HXB/STR YO32 11
Huntington School
HXB/STR YO32 10
ICT@Westfield
RYKW YO26 22
Imphal Barracks
FUL/HES YO10 24
Innkeeper's Lodge
FUL/HES YO10 25
Jorvik
CYK YO1 3
The Joseph Rowntree School
HXB/STR YO32 10
Julia Avenue Retail Park
HXB/STR YO32 11
The Kings Manor
CYK YO1 2
Knavesmire Manor Hotel
ACOMB YO24 23
Knavesmire Primary School
COP/BISH YO23 23
Lady Ann Middletons Hotel
CYK YO1 2
Lakeside CP School
RAW/SKEL YO30 9
Learning Resources Centre
ACOMB YO24 27
Lendal Tower
CYK YO1 2
Link Business Park
FUL/HES YO10 20
Lord Deramore's Primary School
FUL/HES YO10 25
Magnet Sports Club
TAD LS24 30
Manor CE School
RYKW YO26 16
Mansion House
CYK YO1 2
McArthurglen Designer Outlet Retail Park
RYKS YO19 28

Index - featured places 41

Name	Ref
rchant Adventurers' Hall YK YO1	3 G4
rchant Taylors Hall YK YO1	3 G3
klegate Bar & Museum COMB YO24	2 C6
dlethorpe Hall Hotel OP/BISH YO23	28 B1
field Business Centre YKW YO26	16 C1
thorpe School OP/BISH YO23	23 H2
ster Hotel RAW/SKEL YO30	2 D2
Minster School YK YO1	3 F3
tel Therapeutic Clinic EWTH YO31	3 G2
nk Bar Museum YK YO1	3 G3
nkgate Health Centre EWTH YO31	3 G2
nks Cross Shopping Park XB/STR YO32	11 G3
unt Royale Hotel COMB YO24	23 G2
Mount School COMB YO24	2 A7
ncaster House Heworth Golf Club) EWTH YO31	18 D2
ional Centre for Early Music YK YO1	3 H5
ional Railway Museum & orkshire Wheel YKW YO26	2 B4
v Earswick Primary School XB/STR YO32	10 C3
vspaper Office YK YO1	3 H5
thminster Business Park YKW YO26	16 A3
th York Trading Estate AW/SKEL YO30	9 G3
AW/SKEL YO30	10 A2
otel UL/HES YO10	3 G7
lands Sports Centre COMB YO24	22 C2
Observatory YK YO1	2 D3
on COMB YO24	2 C6
Old School Medical Centre OP/BISH YO23	26 C4
Starre Inn YK YO1	2 E3
aldwick Industrial Estate YKS YO19	20 A4
aldwick Primary School UL/HES YO10	19 H5
Ladys RC Primary School COMB YO24	23 E3
Palace OP/BISH YO23	28 B3
k Grove Primary School EWTH YO31	3 G1

The Physical Therapy Clinic COP/BISH YO23	23 H3
Pike Hills Golf Club COP/BISH YO23	26 C3
Pioneer Business Park RAW/SKEL YO30	9 G3
Poppleton Road Primary School RYKW YO26	17 E4
Premier Travel Inn ACOMB YO24	2 C6
RYKW YO26	8 C5
Purey Cust Nuffield Hospital CYK YO1	2 E2
Ralph Butterfield Primary School HXB/STR YO32	7 E2
Ramada Hotel RAW/SKEL YO30	8 C2
Rawcliffe Infant School RAW/SKEL YO30	9 F5
Red Tower HEWTH YO31	3 J5
Regimental Museum CYK YO1	3 F5
Riding Lights Theatre Co CYK YO1	2 E5
Riverside Caravan & Camping Park RAW/SKEL YO30	28 B3
Riverside Primary School TAD LS24	30 C2
Robert Wilkinson Primary School HXB/STR YO32	5 F2
The Royal York Hotel ACOMB YO24	2 C4
St Aelreds RC VA Primary School HEWTH YO31	19 G4
St Anthony's Hall CYK YO1	3 G3
St Barnabas CE Primary School RYKW YO26	17 G4
St Georges RC Primary School FUL/HES YO10	24 B2
St Josephs RC Primary School TAD LS24	30 C2
St Lawrence CE Primary School FUL/HES YO10	3 K7
St Olave's School RAW/SKEL YO30	2 B2
St Oswalds CE Primary School FUL/HES YO10	24 C5
St Pauls CE Primary School ACOMB YO24	2 A6
St Peter's School CYK YO1	2 C1
St Wilfrids RC Primary School HEWTH YO31	3 G2
St Williams College CYK YO1	3 F3
Selby College CYK YO1	3 F4
TAD LS24	30 D3
The Shopping Precinct COP/BISH YO23	26 C5

Siwards How FUL/HES YO10	25 E2
Skelton Park Trading Estate RAW/SKEL YO30	8 C2
Skelton Primary School RAW/SKEL YO30	8 D1
South Bank Medical Centre COP/BISH YO23	24 A3
Stagecoach Youth Theatre HEWTH YO31	3 G2
Stamford Bridge Medical Centre STMFBR YO41	15 F3
Stamford Bridge Primary School STMFBR YO41	15 F3
Station Business Park RYKW YO26	17 G5
Stockton Hall Hospital HXB/STR YO32	12 D2
Stockton on the Forest Primary School HXB/STR YO32	13 E1
Tadcaster Albion FC TAD LS24	30 D3
Tadcaster CC TAD LS24	30 C3
Tadcaster East Primary School TAD LS24	31 E2
Tadcaster Sports & Leisure Centre TAD LS24	30 C3
Tang Hall Clinic FUL/HES YO10	19 F5
Theatre Royal CYK YO1	2 E3
Thornhill Industrial Estate RYKS YO19	20 D5
Tower Court Business Centre RAW/SKEL YO30	9 G4
Tower Court Health Centre RAW/SKEL YO30	9 H4
Tower House Business Centre FUL/HES YO10	24 B2
Travelodge CYK YO1	3 G6
Treasurer's House CYK YO1	3 F2
University College of Ripon & York (Heworth Croft) HEWTH YO31	3 J1
University of York FUL/HES YO10	25 E2
University of York Sports Centre FUL/HES YO10	25 E3
Walmgate Bar CYK YO1	3 J6
Warner Bros RAW/SKEL YO30	9 H3
Warthill CE Primary School RYKS YO19	13 H3
Westfield Primary Community School ACOMB YO24	22 B2
Whitby Drive Medical Centre HEWTH YO31	19 F2

Wigginton Primary School HXB/STR YO32	6 B2
Windmill House Industrial Estate HXB/STR YO32	6 A1
Woodthorpe Primary School ACOMB YO24	22 C5
Yearsley Grove Primary School HEWTH YO31	11 E5
Yearsley Swimming Baths HEWTH YO31	18 C1
York Castle Museum CYK YO1	3 G6
York City Art Gallery RAW/SKEL YO30	2 D2
York City Crematorium COP/BISH YO23	28 B2
York City FC (Bootham Crescent) RAW/SKEL YO30	18 A3
York City Knights RLFC (Huntington Stadium) HXB/STR YO32	11 E4
York City Rowing Club CYK YO1	2 D4
York College ACOMB YO24	27 H1
York County Court CYK YO1	3 G6
York Cricket & RUFC RAW/SKEL YO30	17 G2
York Crown Court CYK YO1	3 F6
York District Hospital RAW/SKEL YO30	18 B2
The York Dungeon CYK YO1	3 F5
York High School ACOMB YO24	22 C2
York Marriott Hotel ACOMB YO24	23 F4
York Minster CYK YO1	3 F3
York Model Railway RYKW YO26	2 B5
York Motor Boat Club House FUL/HES YO10	24 A5
York Racecourse COP/BISH YO23	23 G4
York St John University College HEWTH YO31	3 F1
Yorkshire Museum RAW/SKEL YO30	2 D3
Yorkshire Museum of Farming RYKS YO19	20 C4
York Sixth Form College COP/BISH YO23	27 G2
York Steiner School FUL/HES YO10	24 B3
The York Story CYK YO1	3 F5
Youth Theatre Yorkshire ACOMB YO24	2 C7

Acknowledgements

ools address data provided by Education Direct.

ol station information supplied by Johnsons

way street data provided by © Tele Atlas N.V. Tele Atlas

en centre information provided by

en Centre Association Britains best garden centres

vale Garden Centres

statement on the front cover of this atlas is sourced, selected and quoted a reader comment and feedback form received in 2004

Notes

AA Street by Street QUESTIONNAIRE

Dear Atlas User
Your comments, opinions and recommendations are very important to us. So please help us to improve our street atlases by taking a few minutes to complete this simple questionnaire.

You do not need a stamp (unless posted outside the UK). If you do not want to remove this page from your street atlas, then photocopy it or write your answers on a plain sheet of paper.

Send to: Marketing Assistant, AA Publishing, 14th Floor Fanum House, Freepost SCE 4598, Basingstoke RG21 4GY

ABOUT THE ATLAS...

Please state which city / town / county you bought:

Where did you buy the atlas? (City, Town, County)

For what purpose? (please tick all applicable)

To use in your local area ☐   To use on business or at work ☐

Visiting a strange place ☐   In the car ☐   On foot ☐

Other (please state)

Have you ever used any street atlases other than AA Street by Street?

Yes ☐   No ☐

If so, which ones?

Is there any aspect of our street atlases that could be improved?
(Please continue on a seperate sheet if necessary)

ML154z   continued overleaf

Please list the features you found most useful:

_____
_____

Please list the features you found least useful:

_____
_____
_____

LOCAL KNOWLEDGE...

Local knowledge is invaluable. Whilst every attempt has been made to make the information contained in this atlas as accurate as possible, should you notice any inaccuracies, please detail them below (if necessary, use a blank piece of paper) or e-mail us at *streetbystreet@theAA.com*

_____
_____
_____

ABOUT YOU...

Name (Mr/Mrs/Ms) _____
Address _____
_____ **Postcode** _____
Daytime tel no _____
E-mail address _____

Which age group are you in?

Under 25 ☐   25-34 ☐   35-44 ☐   45-54 ☐   55-64 ☐   65+ ☐

Are you an AA member?   YES ☐   NO ☐

Do you have Internet access?   YES ☐   NO ☐

_____
_____

Thank you for taking the time to complete this questionnaire. Please send it to us as soon as possible, and remember, you do not need a stamp (unless posted outside the UK).

We may use information we hold about you to, telephone or email you about other products and services offered by the AA, we do NOT disclose this information to third parties.

Please tick here if you do not wish to hear about products and services from the AA. ☐

ML154z